Citizen Mary

A Political Memoir

By Mary Valentine

Citizen Mary

Published by

Splattereinkpress.com

ISBN 978-1-939294-24-1

Dedication

To Team Valentine

Acknowledgments

When I ran for office, so many people helped. I have come to discover it is the same when writing a book: it requires lots of good help.

Thank you to every single one of you who made this journey possible, starting with countless dedicated volunteers and interns, who give generously of their time and talents year after year to bring the priceless gift of good government to the citizens of Michigan. Thanks also to the hard-working organizers who helped get me elected: Sarah Roberts, Mike Blake, Jeff Rector, Jen Patterson, Jeff Winston and Marty. And my deep gratitude to all of the staffers who worked so hard for the constituents of the 91st District during my tenure in office: Chris Kilgroe, Melissa Weipert, Julie Dow, Anne Pawli and Adam Forte. By working so hard every day, you not only made my job easier, the camaraderie we shared made the long days seem shorter.

Thanks goes to my editor, Margaret Willey. We were at a meeting at the Muskegon Heights Library when I casually mentioned I was writing a book about my experiences as a legislator; she casually mentioned she was an editor. A warm and professional friendship was born, and the months of re-writing began. Thank you, Margaret for your work on my raw manuscript, your encouragement to keep the project moving, and your friendship.

Next, off the manuscript went to Jenny Roberts, who proofread the entire book, looking at each word to make sure this work was readable and accurate. Jenny, thank you for your diligence, your professionalism and your encouragement.

Thank you to Tricia L. McDonald and her team at Splattered Ink Press for making the whole thing visually appealing.

Thanks to Branden Gemzer for giving the manuscript the once over and offering good suggestions.

Throughout life, it is always our families who offer that special ingredient called love to make it all worthwhile, so thank you to my family. And to my husband Phil, thank you for your endless patience with me and your encouragement in pursuing yet another time-consuming project.

In memory of:

Kate Ebli

Chris Bedford

Gary Conrad

Introduction

"I hate politics," I've heard too many people say. "It's such a dirty game."

Yes. It can be a dirty game. I should know. I served in the Michigan State Legislature for four years. It all began in 2006 when I ran for the Michigan House of Representatives from the 91st district, winning my first-ever election as a previously unknown Democratic candidate. In addition to serving on the Commerce, Great Lakes and Environment, Health Policy, and Retiree Health Care Reforms Committees, I was vice-chair of the Education Committee, and chair of the Family and Children Services Committee (during my second term). I was as committed to serving the people of Muskegon and Ottawa Counties as I could be. Dirty game? I played for all I was worth.

In 2010, I ran for the open Michigan 34th State Senate seat and lost that election. My previously held House seat also fell to a Republican candidate. That election was quite a contrast to my thrilling earlier two victories in the House. The campaign was brutal—and yes, dirty—and in many ways, I'm still recovering, retired now from both politics and my career as a speech pathologist in the Reeths-Puffer Public Schools.

But I have no regrets. I did what I believed I needed to do to help my district, my state, and my country. When we fail to become involved in politics, when we ignore the dirty game, when we fail to improve the political landscape, we put our liberty at risk. Even before I ran for office, I knew this was true. It's why I think every citizen needs to engage in politics, one way or another, using their time and talents in the ways that best suit them.

Each race I ran was fiercely competitive and hundreds of people helped me. So many deserve my thanks for their support during my campaigns. They did the gritty work of any campaign: talking with voters at their doors, making phone calls, working in precincts on Election Day, helping to put mailers out, donating their hard-earned money, encouraging me along the way. I wish I could mention each and every one of them by name, but there were simply too many! Please know that this book is also my attempt to show my appreciation to my supporters.

There were others, too, who gave me the opportunity to help them solve their problems with the government, banks, insurance companies, and all manner of life challenges. We worked tirelessly together with varying degrees of success. I appreciate each of those dear friends as well.

I met many wonderful people while I was involved in Michigan politics and they're in my thoughts to this day. From the owners of a deer farm in eastern Muskegon County, to folks working to move the S.S. Milwaukee Clipper to downtown Muskegon, to owners of a German battery company hoping to locate in Muskegon Township, to dairy farmers in Muskegon County, to a small business that built lake-side elevators—all these new friends and supporters were a cherished part of my political life. I met hard-working employees walking a picket line at the Muskegon Correction Facility. I met Montague High School's Future Farmers of America. Each event I attended and every person I met became an indelible part of this great adventure: running for office and then serving as a state representative. I've reconstructed many conversations from memory. While I don't have a photographic memory, the gist of these conversations, as well as the impressions they made upon me, is true.

I believe we are at greater risk of losing our rights and liberties now than at any time in our nation's recent history. Voter suppression measures and super PACS are becoming the norm in the political arena. Our middle class is shrinking, while the number of hard-working citizens living and working in poverty has increased. We have the largest prison population of any developed country and our public education system is on the brink of being taken over by corporations that put profits before students. Air, water, and food quality is declining.

Working to solve these problems for our children and grandchildren is our patriotic duty—the responsibility of citizenship in a free country. In 2005, when I first decided to run for office, I knew it was time for me to play a larger role, as a patriot and a citizen. I was inexperienced, uncertain, and sometimes plain scared. But I jumped in anyway. I jumped into the ring and joined the fight to improve our country and protect our freedoms.

Mary Valentine, April, 2014

Table of Contents

Chapter I

Election Day 2010

It is January in Michigan. It's a bitter, snowy month—the first January in many years that I haven't been either running a campaign, or driving back and forth to Lansing to serve in the Michigan House of Representatives. It's a time of reflection, and I do need to reflect. The last six months of my life were a roller coaster of challenges and emotions. I'm only just beginning to come to terms with the ups and downs I've experienced as a result of my unsuccessful Senate race. Now it's over, and I'm back to my life in Norton Shores.

I've found a spot where it feels safe to go over in my mind all that happened—the brutal election as well as the difficult campaign that preceded it. Several mornings a week I come to The Coffee House, a café not far from my home, where I seek out a quiet table and sit with my Acer notebook, my coffee, and my memories. I want to go even farther back, to my days in the legislature. And even farther, to my thrilling House seat elections—both hard-won victories.

And farther still, to my childhood in Bay City, Michigan, where I grew up with a dad who loved to watch the local news, follow the elections, and argue with his brothers and sisters about politics. At my quiet table, where I am just a customer and not an elected official, I can pull together all the strands of my journey.

I've decided to begin with my defeat in November 2010. I need to write about that event while everything is fresh. It may seem strange to start there, but it really was the beginning of where I am today. If I hadn't lost that election, I wouldn't be sitting in a Norton Shores café, writing about my rise and fall in Michigan politics. So let's begin on Election Day: November 2, one of the longest days of my entire life.

* * * *

Voting day began after a sleepless November night at the Norton Shores home I share with my husband, Phil Valentine, and our cat, Cody. At that time, our adult children, Robin and Shawn, still shared our home as well. Remembering that morning, I see myself moving as if in a dream through all the ordinary tasks of preparing for the day. I got up at 5:00 a.m. and had my usual coffee and toast for breakfast. I styled my hair, dressing casually in jeans and a comfortable sweater. It was still dark as I drove out of my neighborhood in my trusty red Vibe to my polling place at Norton Shores City Hall, where I was one of the first people to cast a vote.

I felt the familiar tingle in my gut to see my own name on the ballot.

"Don't say your name out loud, Mary," the poll workers teased. "You don't want to be accused of campaigning in the polling place."

With the most important task of the day completed, I hopped back into my cherry red Chevy Vibe, drove back down Henry Street and onto Norton Avenue to Ben Gillette's campaign headquarters, where we had all spent many hours during the final days of the campaign. Ben Gillette, a bright and promising young candidate, was running for the seat I had vacated to run for State Senate. Our campaigns, along with Marcia Hovey-Wright's campaign for State Representative in the 92nd District, had joined forces at Ben's headquarters for a final get-out-the-vote effort. I greeted campaign supporters who were hard at work and then headed out to Connection Hall in the heart of Muskegon Heights, where several early-morning volunteers were gathering. Suddenly someone realized we needed coffee, so I got back into my car and drove to the Bigsby's Coffee Shop on Henry Street, where I purchased a large urn.

By the time I returned, Connection Hall was buzzing, with 50 or so campaign workers waiting for their coffee. Taking the urn to a long table at the back of the room, I noticed that some kind soul had brought in doughnuts. I began shaking hands with my supporters, feeling grateful for their presence.

"Thank you so much for your work on my behalf today."

"I deeply appreciate your efforts."

"Here, have some coffee."

Soon Patsy Petty came into the hall, wearing a bright blue top, gold hoop earrings, and a big smile—full of her usual pep and verve. Trill Bates was there, too. Quieter than Patsy, she always knew exactly what to do—and did it efficiently. Having someone like Trill on a campaign is essential—you could *always* count on her to get the job done. Patsy and Trill shooed most of the campaign workers out to the streets to begin getting the citizens of Muskegon Heights to the polls.

Throughout the campaign, we'd made a special effort to talk to voters from every corner of the Heights. It's a unique community, severely depressed economically but rich in spirit and religious passion. Churches are everywhere and people are quick to greet you with a blessing or a warm thank you. Some of my most important supporters were from the Heights, and I was always happy to connect with voters there. On that morning, I left Connection Hall and began knocking on doors myself along Sixth Street, telling every person I saw on the street to get out and vote.

I reminded a man I saw getting into his car on Barney Street in Muskegon Heights that it was Election Day.

"Where do I vote?" he asked me.

I put in a quick call to Brad Wilson in Lansing, who looked up the polling place so the man could get to the right spot. Yes, it was one vote—but I wanted him to have it. Of course, I hoped he would vote for me. But I felt more urgency about finding his polling place than about getting his vote.

This Election Day was different from my two previous elections. As I walked through streets and knocked on doors, I felt strangely calm. I kept moving—knocking on doors, introducing myself, and reminding the citizens of Muskegon Heights to cast their votes.

Meanwhile, back in Norton Shores, our home had become a staging area where many volunteers had also been working throughout the day, making final calls to voters. In the late afternoon, I joined my supporters in my own kitchen and began a round of last-minute calling on my own phone. It was 5:00 p.m. and I was tired, but through my tiredness, I felt the same odd sense of calm. I didn't realize it at the time, but looking back, I see that it wasn't a good sign. In years past, Election Day had always filled me with such excitement that I could barely stay inside my skin.

I had an Election Day routine by then—return home late in the afternoon, rest briefly, and then prepare for a long, momentous evening in the spotlight. I had learned that it's important to be well rested when you win an election. Reporters and bloggers want to interview you and you don't want to look disheveled or sound incoherent. If you lose, I was to discover, they don't really want to talk with you; they just want to take your picture.

So after making some calls, I rested a short while, then changed into more professional clothes for the evening ahead. My outfit included pearl earrings that my daughter had given me for Christmas a few years ago and my grandmother's opal wedding ring, which I often wear for good luck on special occasions. That night I put it on with great appreciation for the right to vote—a right my grandmother hadn't been able to enjoy until she was 40 years old.

What would she have thought of all of this, I wondered, my died-in-the-wool Republican grandma? I think she would have been proud of me, despite our different party affiliations. I was always proud to wear her ring. I know my paternal grandmother, the one I never came to know, would have been proud. She, too, was a political organizer, though she did her work through the Grange in Adrian, Michigan, rather than with the Democratic Party in Muskegon.

Democratic headquarters everywhere tend to have a similar look and feel. Half-filled cups of coffee in white Styrofoam cups on folding tables that are scratched and beaten up from years of use, pulled out of someone's basement and donated to the campaign. On every table is at least one phone, with a place set aside for a phone bank. The walls are lined with political posters, including posters of our heroes—John F. Kennedy, Martin Luther King, Jr., George McGovern. Hope and idealism fill the air of a Democratic Headquarters—and Ben Gillette's headquarters fit right in with that scenario.

Earlier that day, the entire headquarters had become a giant food dispensary. Hundreds of volunteers working in precincts across the county needed to be fed throughout the day. The front of the office was the distribution center. In the morning, volunteers had assembled small white boxes filled with juice and bagels, handing them out to runners who took them to precinct workers. Each time a volunteer runner came in, he or she would pile boxes into the back of his or her car and drive off to feed the campaign workers. This continued until all the boxes were gone.

Then it was time to make the lunch boxes, filling them with turkey sandwiches, chips, and cookies. Again, the runners drove food to the workers. It was an incredible organizational feat—the largest in the state—and the pride and joy of my campaign manager, Chris Kilgroe.

Poll challengers, who spent the day at voting sites, marked off identified supporters as they voted. Other volunteers were still making phone calls both from their own homes and from mine, reminding our supporters to get out to the polls. All our calls were human-to-human. No robotic calls (also known as robo-calls) for us. Unlike our Republican opponent, we couldn't afford them, but I never wanted them anyway. I think voters appreciate the personal touch. I've always loved the way live calls make the campaign office buzz with animated voices and high energy throughout the day and into the evening.

Surprisingly, the hope, enthusiasm, and idealism that imbued the campaign never wavered throughout the long day. The polls gave Democrats no reason for hope, but that never matters. The energy required to run a strong campaign is fueled by hope. So even though recent polls were predicting a massive win for Republicans throughout the state and the country, and even though I had been on the receiving end of an unbelievable outpouring of negative advertising, everyone stayed hopeful.

The headquarters included a "War Room," a large room toward the back of the building with a sofa, comfy chairs, and several long tables with folding chairs. Some preferred to call it our "Peace Room," but whatever name was attached, we all knew it was the inner chamber of the campaign on Election Day. Precinct Reporting Forms were tacked up on the walls, ready to receive vote totals from various precincts throughout the district. Shortly after the polls closed, returns began dribbling in.

Former state representative candidate Branden Gemzer, a big supporter and steadfast worker, was keeping track of the numbers, recording them on the appropriate Precinct Reporting Forms on the walls. Branden was a terrific volunteer. He had served in the Marines, including two tours of duty in Iraq—though with his reddish brown hair, goatee, and intelligence, he reminded me more of a college professor than a veteran of war. I'd known him since 2008, when I was running for my second term as state representative and he was running for township supervisor of Egleston Township. Branden was irreplaceable—smart, energetic, and ethical— just the type of person you would like to represent you in public office. That night he hung in there, recording vote totals until every last vote was counted. I will never forget his loyalty.

At 8:00 p.m., I wound my way through the labyrinth of rooms to a quiet spot in the back of the building, where a reporter from WZZM in Grand Rapids had requested an interview. I don't remember his name and have no idea what I said. I just remember looking into the camera and feeling such a mix of emotions—stress, appreciation for my staff, and relief. Yes, relief. It had been a grueling campaign. Soon it would be over. My opponent, Goeff Hansen, had broadcast one big lie and many distortions about me. He had even brought a ridiculous lawsuit against me. I knew I would no longer have to defend myself against his claims about me, and I was glad.

But another part of me was not quite ready to admit defeat. After the WZZM interview, I crept into the War Room to peek at a few of the voter tabulation sheets taped to the walls. When I saw the returns from Dalton Township, I knew immediately I was done. I read the returns from Cedar Creek just to verify, and saw the same lack of Democratic votes. There would be no way to recover from such heavy losses in those Democratic strongholds. The only thing left was to watch more gruesome numbers trickle in. And they *were* gruesome: more precincts, more numbers, more proof of defeat. The extent of my loss came into sharp focus. It was a landslide victory for my Republican opponent.

I would need to somehow put my emotions aside to make it through the rest of this very public evening.

Back in the "War Room," I sank into one of the comfy chairs and noticed the WZZM reporter was back—this time with a still camera. Standing about four feet from my face, he snapped frame after frame. My usually genuine smile turned into one pasted on for his benefit. Away he snapped. Finally, between clenched teeth, I whispered to no one in particular, "Make this man go away."

Chris, my friend and campaign manager, was watching this disaster unfold as well, and when he heard my request he approached the photographer.

"You need to leave now," he said. Thankfully, the reporter stopped snapping pictures and walked right out the front door.

Chris is 6 feet 4 inches tall with a shock of curly brown hair and a boyish smile that disguises his 50-something age. Perhaps on that night he felt somewhat responsible for getting me into the Senate race—though he didn't need to feel that way. I'm a grown woman, and running for state senator was my own decision. But he had encouraged me, in part because he knew better than anyone what I was capable of. He knew I would give it my all from beginning to end and would serve the constituents honorably as a state senator.

Chris and I made an odd pair. He's tall; I'm short. I'm extremely cautious; he can be reckless. He never forgets a name; I never remember a name. It was a peculiar but effective political partnership. "Mary Valentine is the best boss a guy could have," I'd heard him say more than once.

My first encounter with a photographer that night wouldn't be my last. Perhaps because of my usual wide smile and sunny disposition, I am quite certain the photographers and reporters couldn't wait to catch me in tears. I remembered that, years ago, on another election night, the *Muskegon Chronicle* had printed a huge close-up of a woman who had lost this very seat—and she was in tears. I still remember that picture displayed prominently on the front page, and how wrong it had seemed that she had been so exposed in her time of defeat. Now I was determined they wouldn't print a similar photo of me. No tears on the front page of the *Chronicle*, or the *Ludington Daily News*, or any TV station.

My tears needed to be tucked away. I knew I would be dealing with them in the weeks and months to come, but on election night, my goal was to get through the evening calmly and with dignity. There was still much to do. A "victory" party was taking shape only a few blocks away at the Polish Union Hall. I knew friends and family were already there. Chris and I drove to the party together.

Once inside the heavy doors of the Hall, I saw the most comforting sight. My mother, Phyllis Hostetler, along with my sisters, Vicki and Maggie, and my brother, Doug, were sitting together at one long table with spouses, partners and children, eating from paper plates, drinking, talking, and laughing. Robin and Shawn were there, along with their significant others: Ren Barnes (now Ren Valentine and my daughter-in-law), and Phil Lurry (now my son-in-law). My beloved family cheered my name when they caught sight of me.

Other tables and other supporters began to cheer for me as well. Jeremy Martin, who had felt like a second son to me when he was in the youth group I sponsored years earlier, was there as well. I truly felt the gang was all here! I smiled—and this time it was a real smile. Here was an oasis and a reward: a gathering of family and the friends I had made during these campaigns, the dear and loyal people who had been with me through thick and thin, hot weather and cold, good news and bad. Suddenly all I wanted in the world was to thank them. I was overcome with gratitude—I literally couldn't wait to get my hands on a microphone.

Somehow, I found the words to thank them, to tell them what their support had meant to me. Thank you, thank you, thank you and thank you— for believing in me, for helping me, for staying with me, for standing beside me on this difficult night.

Then it was time to join my family. I appreciated their energy and their love. One family member was absent though—an important one: my wonderful husband, Phil. Sometimes I think the tough campaign, including all the lies, accusations, and insults, was hardest on him. He's a protective person by nature, and he had to watch me endure so much. He had seen the writing on the wall concerning my campaign long before anyone else, and yet had remained my strongest supporter. I literally couldn't have stayed in the campaign without him. Still, we had decided that it might be easier for both of us if he were out of town on election night. He would have especially hated the photographers trying to get pictures of me in defeat mode. So I gave him my blessing: Skip the "victory" party.

While talking with Doug, I noticed a *Chronicle* photographer standing three feet in front of me, snapping picture after picture of my face. And I realized all in a flash that I didn't have to put up with this sort of treatment anymore. I would no longer be in the public eye—no longer be forced to wear a smile as I tolerated rudeness from the press. I turned my back to the photographer and resumed my conversation with my brother. The photographer walked around me, put his camera in my face again and continued snapping. Again, I turned my back to him. Again he moved to face me, the camera aimed at my face. Click. Click. Click.

"You need to leave now," I said. To my amazement, he did! I felt such elation. I turned to Doug and admitted, "I'm grateful to have my life back."

Suddenly it was 10:00 p.m. and time to celebrate the end of the campaign. My good friend and campaign worker Anne Pawli had brought tequila for the celebration. My drinking days were in the distant past, but if there was ever a night for straight shots, this was it. Someone from my ever-competent, loyal staff ran for the salt. They reminded me how to combine it with the straight shot for the best antidote to a losing campaign. Together we toasted ourselves—our finished campaign and our lasting friendships.

Many returns had come in from around the state. Dan Scripps, top-notch Democratic representative in the district north of us, went down, and so did Jennifer Haas, the most dedicated state representative in the House. Deb Kennedy. Terry Brown. Kate Ebli, Marty Griffin, Mike Lahti, Kathleen Law. All great legislators. All Democrats. All voted out of office. It was a massive loss for the Democratic Party—and the citizens—in Michigan and across the country. My reaction to this news was mixed. I was heartbroken to have so many strong Democrats out of office and to lose our majority in the House of Representatives. But to be perfectly honest, it took some of the sting out of the night to know I didn't lose my election alone. I was part of a sweeping political shift.

The night wore on. Near its end my beloved daughter, Robin, received a call from the *Ludington Daily News*. Robin had been so important to my campaign; the bonding that took hold between us was one of the campaign's greatest gifts. Robin is a beautiful and charming woman, but her teen

My daughter Robin and I on Election Night '08 – at the headquarters in front of the voter tabulation sheets.

years had been tough for both of us. The campaign had erased all of our earlier conflict. Robin's sense of humor and support had buoyed me up more than a few times in the past months. Seeing your mother treated as I had been treated during the campaign would be an ordeal for any child. But Robin was strong. She waved to me and cried, "Mom! A *Ludington Daily News* photographer wants to meet with you!"

"Tell him 'No thanks,'" I called back to her. "No more damn photographers tonight."

My staff cheered.

"Mary Valentine is not available to see you," Robin told the photographer, her voice polite but firm.

"I didn't ask whether she was available," he replied, "I asked where she was."

That was the wrong thing to say to Robin—after the long months of watching the attacks of her mom, the misrepresentations and sometimes downright lies. Not to mention the tequila! She ended that conversation quickly. The same man had the nerve to call back and announce that he had driven from Ludington to Muskegon and claim I'd promised to see him on election night—though I certainly didn't remember promising any such thing.

"Mom," Robin reported. "He says he's coming anyway."

It was late—the hall was mostly cleared out. "Get me out of here, then," I asked my family and staff. My steadfast team went into action. Branden, former Marine and loyal supporter, took charge of standing guard at the front door. Robin and her boyfriend, Phil, our designated driver for the evening, whisked me out the back door and drove me home.

It was 2:00 a.m. when my head finally hit the pillow. *I'm officially out of politics,* I told myself. It still didn't seem real. Yet it was real. I knew that I would wake up the next morning to a different reality, both politically and personally. I knew I would have to face my disappointment about who would be running our state. I felt the full force of my defeat.

Chapter II

Sixth Street

I am back at the café, thinking about my friend Kate Ebli. Kate and I both lost our elections in the Republican deluge of 2010, or what Kirsten Bremer called "a landslide of stupidity." I remember sitting in the House chamber with Kate after the election, discussing the best way to say our final goodbyes to our colleagues in the state legislature. Her response was classic Kate.

"If I were to say something," she told me, "it would be this: 'as a state legislator, I have met the best and most dedicated people I could ever hope to meet. I have also met the opposite. You decide which of these two you are.'"

Then she'd sit down.

I felt the same.

The number of wonderful people I met on this job is too great for me to mention them all by name: the people who worked to change harmful public policy when they experienced personal tragedy, the legislators who did everything in their power to meet the needs of their constituents and freely gave time away from their families to do so, the union folks who gave generously of their time to advocate for their friends and colleagues, and all the campaign workers who made success-ful campaigns happen.

Of course, there were the political hacks I served with, too—more about them later. Right now, I need to stay positive.

I knew that remembering the superb friends I had made in my time in politics would speed up the healing process. Months of introspection and self-evaluation lay ahead of me. How had I come to put myself in this situation? How was I supposed to make sense of the fact that Goeff Hansen and the Republican Party had spent something like $1 million defeating me with their dirty campaign—that their tactics had outweighed all my dedicated service? What forces had brought me to this point?

A good place to start is on Sixth Street in Bay City, Michigan, my childhood home.

* * * *

Our barn-like yellow house in Bay City, Michigan, was big enough for the Hostetler family—five kids, a fox terrier named Christopher, and our parents, Bob and Phyl Hostetler. In the fifties, families of this size and even bigger were the norm. Our home was one of those lovely, old-fashioned houses with a well-used porch swing at one end of a wide front porch. Sixth Street was lined with trees and crawling with kids. For us kids, friends were always ready to play kick the can or capture the flag after dark, and afternoons were busy with baseball games and walks to Carroll Park to feed the ducks. I like to say that my childhood was Bay City's version of *Leave It to Beaver.*

My father had majored in history at Adrian College. He'd served in the Navy during WWII and worked as a journalist at the *Bay City Times.* Bob Hostetler was definitely a man who loved politics. I can still see him, watching the TV news every night of my early childhood from his easy chair, surrounded by the daily newspapers he read. He never actually ran for office, walked in a Memorial Day parade, or gave a stump speech, but he was always deeply engaged in both the local and national news of the day, and always willing to debate any issue—especially with his four siblings. You could call him a passionate armchair politician.

My mother was the activist—not so much in politics, but in every other arena. Phyl Hostetler loved to get involved. If we wanted to join the Girl Scouts, she became the leader. If a teacher was needed for Sunday school, she was there Sunday mornings, Bible in hand. Her degree from Michigan State University was in Home Economics and she used her skills well. She was a fully engaged mother—she sewed our clothes, canned fruit for the winter months, baked bread and cookies on Saturday mornings, and served a nightly feast of a dinner at 6:00 p.m. each evening, dependable as the sunrise. Unlike Dad, she didn't have much patience for long political discussions. *Do something about it or keep quiet* would have been her motto back then. She frequently complained when Dad and his siblings discussed world news. *It's like arguing about the salt mines in Siberia,* she'd say about those Hostetler family debates.

I was lucky to have a childhood like that. There wasn't much extra money, but my parents managed their household with common sense and wisdom about what mattered— home-cooked meals, handmade clothes, music lessons, and an annual splurge—vacationing at a lakeside cottage up north, never the same cottage twice. My dad saved a small amount of money each week to cover the cost of our vacations. We learned to save from him. We each had a small allowance and found jobs as soon as we were old enough. And always, always, they emphasized the importance of a good education.

Together, they influenced my life and my own brand of activism. My mother made it impossible for me to sit by and watch our government run aground, as I believe it had during George W. Bush's presidency. Like Mom, I knew I had to jump in with both feet and do something besides complain. But even before that, my father's influence made it impossible for me to ignore the importance of politics in our everyday lives. Like him, I was always interested in local, state, and federal government and the ways in which laws affected people. I wanted to be an informed citizen, as he had been, with strong opinions that I was not afraid to express.

But truthfully, I was a timid girl—the middle child in my family—quiet as a mouse. My mom would conspire with my teachers all through my elementary school years to get me to speak in class. Nothing worked; I simply wouldn't talk. In high school, and even in college, I dreaded any class that depended on class participation. It was a lot of work for me to manage to speak up once or twice a marking period to keep my grades up. Luckily, I had many wonderful teachers. The public schools in Bay City were excellent—one of the reasons my parents had relocated there from Flint when I was one year old.

The other reason was that my dad landed a job at the *Bay City Times*. Ultimately we ended up in the Sixth Street neighborhood, just a few blocks from Washington School, a turn-of-the-century K-8 building where I began my education. We sat at little desks with inkwells and learned to read and write. From there I went to Bay City Central High School, followed by Delta College and Central Michigan University. I earned my Master's degree in Education from Northern Michigan University.

Good public education was important to my parents, which is part of the reason I am sickened by the disintegration of public schools I am witnessing every day around our state and nation. Both my grandmothers valued a college education more than silver and gold, and passed those values on to both my parents, who passed them along to me. This, I believe, is part of why I am such a passionate supporter of public education today.

Other influences affected me. An important one was my growing awareness of the injustice and inequality that African-Americans dealt with on a daily basis—in my hometown, my home state, and across the country.

For white, middle-class families like mine, the fifties were an idyllic time, prosperous and full of opportunities. But the underbelly of Eden, already well known to our African-American citizens, had begun to reveal itself to the white community. Emmitt Till, an African-American teenager from Chicago, was brutally beaten and murdered for flirting with a white woman in Mississippi. His mother, Mamie Till, chose to have an open casket at his funeral and invited *Jet Magazine* to take photos of the murdered boy. These terrible images flashed across the country. Soon afterward, Rosa Parks of Montgomery, Alabama, stood up for herself instead of standing up for a white man on a bus. African-Americans began to demand their civil rights as American citizens. They refused to ride city buses if they had to sit at the back. They staged protest sit-ins and marches. Freedom rides—busloads of college students demanding equal rights for minorities—proliferated throughout the South until those ugly "whites only" signs came down.

While a teenager, I read *Black Like Me* (originally published in 1961), by John Howard Griffen. The author, a white man, disguised himself as an African-American when Jim Crow laws were in effect in the south. Once Griffen had changed his racial identity, he was often unable to find a place to eat or even use public bathrooms, and he was treated with verbal abuse and ridicule. This book changed my life and opened my eyes to the deep racial fissure that divided us then—and divides us still. It was another kind of education.

As I write this, the news is covering the story of a young African-American boy, Trayvon Martin, who was walking home from the store, minding his own business, when a self-appointed neighborhood watch captain named George Zimmerman, armed with a handgun, followed Trayvon, shot, and killed him. Initially, Zimmerman walked away a free man—no arrest, no inquiry, and no trial. Florida's "stand your ground" law was used as the excuse to let Zimmerman walk free. After a huge national uproar on the dead boy's behalf, Zimmerman was arrested. As I write this, he's awaiting trial. It's a tragic example of how the struggle for justice and equal treatment under the law continues into the twenty-first century.[1] It's also an example of what happens when legislators write and enact bad laws, and when we the people don't pay attention to what our legislature is doing.

My political activism started with George McGovern's campaign for the presidency in 1972. At the time I lived in Iron Mountain, a small town on U.S. Highway 2, halfway between Mackinac Island and Ironwood in Michigan's wild and wonderful Upper Peninsula. Iron Mountain was born, as the name implies, when iron was king in the Upper Peninsula. The area was surrounded by dense forests. Snow was deep and constant in the bitterly cold winters, and springtime was sweeter as a result. I campaigned for George

---

[1] Ultimately, Zimmerman was found not guilty and walked free. I am sorry to report that many people were quick to blame Martin, although he was merely walking home from the store.

McGovern as a young woman, knocking on doors in the North End of Iron Mountain, a Democratic stronghold. It was exciting to be part of that political drama and a good history lesson as well.

Often when I asked voters if they would be supporting McGovern, they would answer: "I haven't voted for a Republican since Hoover, and I don't intend to start now." This was my first introduction to the legacy of Herbert Hoover.

After the election, I became involved in the Dickinson County Democratic Party. Eventually, I became the vice chair, and even served on the Democratic Party's State Central Committee for a time.

Later, shortly after the Watergate mess, the local prosecutor in Iron Mountain, a Democrat named Frannie Brouillette, launched a campaign for Congress against then-Congressman Phil Ruppe. Frannie gave me a part-time job as his scheduler—my first paid political job. I loved every moment of it. It was a good year to be a young Democrat, with Democratic candidates sweeping into office across the land. Unfortunately, Frannie Brouillette lost by a thin hair.

Soon after this initial campaign experience, my first husband and I divorced. I went on to graduate school at Northern Michigan University in Marquette. There I met Phil Valentine, to whom I have been married since 1979. Together we relocated, first to Grand Rapids and eventually to Muskegon, Michigan, a city on another inland sea, Lake Michigan. From the moment I first drove into Muskegon, it felt like home, reminding me of Bay City. While Phil and I raised our family—our two beautiful children, Robin and Shawn—I put my activism aside and continued my professional life as a speech pathologist in the public school system, traveling to different schools in the Muskegon area to work with young children struggling with delayed speech and language skills.

21

I started paying attention to politics again during the 2000 election, when George W. Bush and Vice President Al Gore were essentially tied in the race for president. Becoming deeply embroiled in the process, I studied past and present elections while the battle raged on, lawsuits were brought, and votes were counted and recounted. It was such a disturbing election cycle and so disheartening for Democrats. Glued to the television for weeks, I watched George W. Bush's cohorts on TV yelling, interrupting people, and telling half-truths—and outright lies. Like the majority of Americans, I was astonished by the Bush supporters' actions and behavior. Eventually, they lied and bullied their way right into the White House, and George W. Bush became our president.

Before we knew it, the horror of 9/11 was upon us, and it was crucial to pull together in its aftermath. Clearly, though, the world was angry with us, not because they were jealous of our freedoms—an idea our leaders tried to convince us of—but because of our thoughtless behavior around the world. We had pulled out of the Kyoto Treaty, acted with increasing arrogance overseas, and squandered the natural resources that we should have been sharing with other countries. After the tragedy of 9/11, I felt that as a nation we had a responsibility to figure out why so many countries hated us and considered us dangerous. I believed we needed to find ways to regain our standing as a respected and generous country. The seeds of my activism were planted in those days.

Then, to my dismay, the Bush administration used the terrorist attacks on the World Trade Centers and the Pentagon as an excuse to invade Iraq, a country that had absolutely nothing to do with 9/11. Our president called this initiative "Shock and Awe." I was outraged at this unnecessary war on a people that had not been responsible for the loss of life on 9/11. All I could think about in those first months of the Iraq war were the young Americans we were putting in harm's way and the innocent civilians that were dying.

We could have used some humility from our president in those terrible days. Instead, President Bush claimed victory after a few weeks, wearing a flight suit as he strutted around like a proud peacock on the deck of the USS Abraham Lincoln, an aircraft carrier stationed off the California coast. The stunt was both expensive for taxpayers and insulting to those who think war, even when necessary, should never be glorified in this way. And he was wrong to declare victory. The war continued, despite increasing evidence that it had been initiated on false pretenses. In August 2011, we still had troops in Iraq. Thousands of people lost lives, limbs, and peace of mind. Not surprisingly, weapons of mass destruction were never found.[2]

The middle class and the poor had more losses to weather. Tax cuts put in place for the wealthiest Americans caused huge deficits. All the progress we had made in the previous decade to clean up our air and water faded. President Bush's education policy, called *No Child Left Behind*, was, in my opinion, a cynical initiative that had nothing to do with improving education, but everything to do with devaluing teachers.

The George W. Bush presidency created a world in which the rich were thriving while the middle class struggled. Poverty rose while schools and teachers were both more burdened and less valued. At one point, my husband, Phil, urged me to read Al Franken's bestselling book, *Lies and the Lying Liars Who Tell Them*. Although Franken's book title was

---

[2] According to *U.S.A. Today*, the Iraqi War formally ended on December 15, 2011.

insulting to many, the book emphasized how far we had been led astray by myths and falsehoods. Shortly after I read this book, I received an invitation to attend a viewing of the film *The Truth About the Iraqi War*, produced by Robert Greenwald. The showing was at the home of Rae Jean Erickson, who lived on Bard Road in North Muskegon. As I drove to her house, I felt in my bones a reconnection to my political history in the Upper Peninsula. The Erickson driveway was already filled with cars, and I read an array of bumper stickers: "No War." "Vote Kucinich." "War Is Not the Answer."

I knew instantly that I was right where I needed to be.

What I learned from Greenwald's documentary shocked and disturbed me. The film revealed the series of calculated lies that had led us into war: Iraq had weapons of mass destruction; Iraq had biological weapons; Iraq was in the process of making atomic weapons. None of it was true, and our leaders knew it. The Bush administration went so far as to reveal the identity of C.I.A. agent Valerie Plame. To some this even seemed like an act of treason. In so doing, our leaders put Plame and other agents' lives at risk. Americans, including most of the media, conveniently looked the other way.

Later, some friends and I started a group called "People for Change." We were committed to getting some of what we had learned into the public discourse. We scheduled Greenwald's film to be shown at local colleges, libraries, and churches.

We also felt the public needed to see some of the other Robert Greenwald films coming out: *Unprecedented,* a movie that followed what really went on behind the scenes during the 2000 presidential election; *Outfoxed*, about Fox News' lack of journalistic integrity, and *The High Cost of Low Prices*, a documentary exposing Wal-Mart's terrible labor practices.

The discussions in which I participated after viewing these films were always energizing.

I became deeply involved in John Kerry's run for president and my political activism returned in full force. With other Kerry supporters, I knocked on doors, made phone calls, walked in parades, and got the vote out on Election Day. We were determined to elect John Kerry and believed he could win. That campaign was the birthplace of a rich collaboration of allies that eventually led to my campaign for state representative.

But then on November 2, 2004, Kerry lost the election to George W. Bush. We were devastated, but many of us were equally appalled by the results of one particular local election: David Farhat, the state representative in the 91st District, won reelection in what many of us thought was a dishonorable campaign.

Farhat was a local developer with a great deal of charm and charisma. He had grown up in a political family, which gave him excellent name recognition in Muskegon County, and he knew how to run a successful campaign. His Democratic opponent was Nancy Frye, an extremely ethical woman who had served for years as a County Commissioner. The state Republican Party, on behalf of David Farhat, made all sorts of wild accusations about Nancy to mislead voters. They accused her of taking junkets on taxpayer money because she represented our community at an event with Muskegon's sister city, Omuta, Japan. In truth there was no better person to represent Muskegon in Omuta. And because, as County Commissioner, Frye had voted for industrial-strength, rather than cheap, office machines, Farhat's campaign had accused her of wasting taxpayers' money.

But here was the clincher: To get Farhat elected, the Republican Party found a picture of Nancy Frye with a small glass in her hand and paired this image with words to make her appear to be a lush—and on taxpayer money, to boot. The truth was that Nancy Frye didn't drink alcohol. And David Farhat never disavowed this trashy ad—nor did he apologize for its implications. He won his second term anyway.

It was clear that someone had to stand up to him in 2006.

The 91st District is an oddly shaped, gerrymandered district that makes a big backward "C" around the city of Muskegon. The district includes many outlying cities and townships, and at that time even included one township in Ottawa County—Chester Township. The Muskegon Democrats knew that it was going to be tough to find someone willing to take on this difficult race.

Shortly after the 2004 election, I was driving down Sherman Boulevard on my way to work, wracking my brain to come up with the right person to challenge David Farhat—someone who was known both in the northern and southern parts of the county. I lived in Norton Shores, south of Muskegon proper, but I worked in the Reeths-Puffer Schools to the north. Suddenly, the solution hit me right between the eyes.

I was that person.

At first, I couldn't even tell anyone that this idea had occurred to me. How could I, an educator with no political experience, even consider running for state representative? The idea began to seem more and more ridiculous. I decided to forget it and tucked the idea safely away in the back of my mind. But I did have one crucial caveat: *if anyone else ever brings it up with me up as a possibility, I might reconsider it.*

That was my state of mind a few weeks later, as I was serving Sunday breakfast to some of my friends from the

Kerry campaign—Pete and Patty Bennett and Chris Kilgroe. We sat around the round oak table in my kitchen, eating French toast and sipping hot coffee, when Chris, a strong political ally, asked me if I had ever considered running for state representative myself. I didn't say no. I admitted I had considered it. That was the beginning.

Chapter III

The Hem and the Haw

Another bittersweet memory comes to me as I sit alone in the café:

It's early November 2010 just after the election, a day filled with goodbyes. I'm at the House Office Building in Lansing on my way to my last Children and Family Services Committee meeting, when Brenda Lawson, a policy analyst, rushes over to me, her hand outstretched to shake mine.

"I want you to know," she says, "that it was an honor to work with you and I consider you a true stateswoman."

Tears sting my eyes, but I manage a smile. Brenda was in the chamber on a night during which I had cast a difficult vote. I believed it was the right thing to do, but also knew it might cost me the next election. Brenda remembered that vote—a tough vote that had left a strong impression on her.

Later that same morning, I talk with my colleagues, Representatives Lesia Liss and Dian Slavens, reviewing all we've accomplished on the Family and Children's Services Committee together. They both thank me warmly for my work as chair of this committee, which was so dear to my heart. This time I can't hold back the tears.

Remembering their thanks, their appreciation for my service, I blink back a few stray tears over my coffee and continue writing.

* * * *

I pondered my decision to run for months. I hemmed, hawed, and agonized. One minute I was ready to announce my plan. The next minute, it seemed a ridiculous idea. How could I be so bold as to think I could be a state lawmaker? I was inexperienced in the areas of law, business, and government—and I hated public speaking. I'm terrible at remembering names. The negatives came rushing to the surface whenever I had a moment to reflect. And yet, every time I decided that running was impossible, something would happen, someone would say something, or I would see another benefit to at least trying. I simply couldn't push the idea away.

For the next several months, I thought about running for office constantly. I went about my normal daily routine as my feelings gradually shifted from uncertainty to determination. I jumped into my white mini-van each weekday, a cup of hot coffee in my carrier, and drove through Muskegon to McMillan Elementary School on Hyde Park Road. There I worked with three-to-eight-year-olds in an unheated storage room, bringing the gift of communication to children who needed it. But now I was considering the possibility of doing something very different.

"How can I possibly run for office?" I asked my daughter, Robin. "I've never owned my own business and David Farhat is a pro in that area."

"He doesn't know anything about education, though," Robin replied. "You're the expert there. And besides, you're smart. You can learn what you need to know about business."

Good point, Robin. Was I an expert in the area of education? I had certainly become convinced that our representatives in Lansing were *not* experts—they appeared to know nothing about our embattled public education system. Few had ever managed a classroom full of rambunctious kids. As a speech pathologist, I didn't face that scenario every day. But I had faced it often enough to develop deep appreciation for those who could do it so well. I could recognize the daily stress those teachers face, and the talent it takes to master that skill.

Our legislators were drafting and proposing laws to get rid of tenure, which wouldn't improve public education one iota, in my opinion. They also wanted merit pay for teachers, a proven policy failure. Providing schools of choice was yet another wrong-headed solution. Ideology had trumped effectiveness and common sense in Michigan's legislature with regard to schools and teachers. It was clear that Lansing needed the input of an educator.

Could I be that educator?

I knew from watching Farhat's campaign against Nancy Frye that this campaign would be a tough one. I knew what might be ahead of me. I worried that my good name in the community would be ruined. I worried about making enemies. I worried about people sneering at me at the grocery store.

We could always move, I told myself. *I've started over many times in my life, and I guess I could do it again.*

I needn't have worried about being hounded out of the community. My first campaign had the opposite result. And once elected, I used the power of my position to help many deserving people, for which I received deep appreciation. Instead of dirty looks at the grocery store, I received handshakes and thanks.

But that came later. In early 2005, I was still unsure, still torn.

I studied the history of the district. The 91st had moved

back and forth from Democrat to Republican since 1988, when our family had relocated to Muskegon. So I knew it was possible for a Democrat to win in this district. I also knew that David Farhat, the incumbent, had eked out two exceedingly close elections—first in 2002 and then again in 2004—which made him vulnerable. He didn't spend enough time in the district and had an undeniable reputation in Muskegon for running dirty campaigns. I wondered if these qualities might weaken him as an opponent in 2006.

Farhat had many strengths, though. He's a naturally gregarious man, and when people meet him for the first time, they can't help liking him. And he was a life-long resident of Muskegon with excellent name recognition—he had been born into a well-known political family. Ironically, his father was a long-time Democrat and his sister, Debbie Farhat, also had previously served one term as a Democratic state representative in the 91st district. In addition, the entire family was deeply involved in Muskegon Catholic Central and its football organization. They had lots of church and school supporters. Many people believed that it was impossible to defeat a Farhat in Muskegon County.

I kept pondering.

In the spring of 2005, I started to raise the subject of a run for political office with a few close friends and relatives. I admit I was afraid my loved ones would laugh at the idea—another unfounded fear. No one laughed; I received only encouragement.

I reminded myself that I was living in a democracy, and in a democracy everyone has a right to run for office. If a citizen thinks he or she has something to offer that the country needs, it becomes more than a right. It becomes a duty.

I did think I had something to offer. For one thing, many of the legislators in Lansing were practicing what seemed to me to be a negative approach to governing. They were bashing gays, unions, and teachers at a time when people needed positive ideas and visionary leadership. Unemployment was high, lack of adequate healthcare coverage was forcing citizens into bankruptcy, home foreclosures were on the rise, and the state economy was a mess. And our "leaders" were introducing legislation to ensure that gays and lesbians wouldn't be able to determine what would happen to their own remains after they died. These same leaders also wanted to strangle our education system and give tax breaks to the wealthiest citizens at the expense of the most vulnerable.

These were hardly well thought out policies for the common good. Certainly I could do better than that.

Many evenings that spring, I discussed the pros and cons of running for office with my husband, Phil, and our children over take-out pizza. Politically, the members of my family were all on the same page. None of us believed the war in Iraq was justifiable, nor did we feel that criminalizing abortion would solve anything—two hot-button issues of the time. We all agreed that we needed stronger policies to protect clean air and water. We all believed in a fair day's pay for a full day's work. We cared about safety at the workplace and everyone paying their fair share of taxes. These were the beliefs that made us a family of Democrats.

We didn't have any idea what we were getting into. We knew as much about running a political campaign as we knew about flying to the moon. But we were in agreement that I should try, if it was what I wanted. Neither my children nor my husband would stand in my way. They told me I was needed in Lansing and they would be by my side every step of the way.

One sunny afternoon in June, I consulted my minister at the time, Julie Armour. We met for lunch at the Main Street

Café, on the deck overlooking Muskegon Lake. I shared with Julie one of my deepest concerns—how running for office might impact my 30-year marriage.

"Mary, if this is something in your heart," she wisely told me, "it will be far worse on your marriage if you *don't* do it."

Ironically, I had published an article years earlier in *Unity Magazine* in which I had made this exact point. I wrote about my belief that each of us has our own unique gifts for which the world is waiting. If they are never given, never realized, it can lead to depression and illness. Remembering that article and the message it now held for me, along with Julie's wise advice, took me one step closer to my decision.

I'm sure some in my extended family—those who had known me since childhood—thought I had lost my mind. They remembered me as an extremely quiet, overly sensitive girl and saw me as an adult version of that girl. They couldn't imagine me weathering the storm of a tough campaign, especially if things got nasty.

In moments of reflection, I wondered if they were right. Was I too sensitive for politics? Too quiet? Too private? I wanted to be perfect for this job. Internally I was creating a list of my flaws and past mistakes. Suddenly, it occurred to me that I was being ridiculous. Perfection was not a job requirement. *You're not running to become God for crying out loud!* I said to myself. *You're running to be a state representative!*

I needed one more person's opinion—my longtime friend, Cynthia George (not her real name). I had such deep respect for her opinions. Smart and perceptive, she had known me many years. Of course I procrastinated, afraid of what she might tell me. But finally, late one afternoon in May, I gathered up all my courage and called her.

I'll never forget that conversation. Alone in my bedroom, I

sat in the wicker chair overlooking a window to my back-yard—the same chair where I would soon begin making fundraising calls for my campaign. With an uncertain voice, I asked my old friend if she thought the idea of running for office had even one iota of sense to it.

"Mary, you'd be a fantastic state representative," she said, without hesitation. I heard the support and approval in her voice loud and clear. Her words pulled me out of those weeks of indecision. If Cynthia believed in me, I would go for it.

Now all I had to do was figure out where to begin!

Chapter IV

Ready, Set ...

A memory: It's the second Thursday in December 2010, and we're gathered at the CIO Hall for the first Democratic Party meeting since the election. Portraits of labor leaders line three walls of the large entryway. These are the same leaders who consistently go to bat for those who do the work of our society: builders, plumbers, electricians, laborers, and steel workers—the ones who make this country tick. Some in our society would kick those workers to the side of the road and call their leaders "union thugs." I call them heroes. I am honored to have known personally so many of them.

The Hall is home to labor meetings of all stripes and also is the rallying spot for protests and rallies. It's a space rich in Muskegon's labor movement history. I'm here to give my final speech as a state representative to my closest friends in the Democratic Party. Speaking in the CIO hall was always a challenge for me, with my soft voice and short stature, but tonight it's wonderful to be here. I speak briefly, thanking them all. When I'm finished, Ida Smith (who, along with her husband Doug, is one of the most committed Democrats I know) gives a small speech thanking me for my work in the House on behalf of the citizens of Michigan.

Now these hard-working and committed Democrats all join in, giving me a standing ovation—and it's especially heartwarming. I'm deeply touched.

The CIO Hall in downtown Muskegon, a home to labor unions.
Inside, pictures of the brave men and women who have
been labor leaders in Muskegon.

* * * *

I was so inexperienced about how to begin my campaign
that I bought myself a book titled: *How To Win A Local
Election.* A step-by-step guide for the uninitiated by Judge
Lawrence Grey, it quickly became my bible. I read it cover to
cover—and even memorized significant sections. One of the
first things I learned from the book was that I needed something called a "voter file."

Making some calls, I discovered the person with whom I
needed to talk about voter files was Lansing's own Mark Fisk,
the Democratic House Caucus Communications Director. It
took me awhile to find him, but I persisted, telling him I was
serious in my plans to run for state representative of the 91st
District.

We set up an appointment at the "offsite" in Lansing, an

ancient, two-story building on Pennsylvania Ave. with many small offices and an abundance of telephones, coffee mugs, and political posters. When Phil and I arrived at the offsite that day in July, we knew without a doubt that our journey had begun. We had left behind our world of landlines, desktop computers, and privacy. We were entering a world of smart phones, laptops, and photo ops. Nothing would be the same.

I chuckle when I picture myself on that day. I wanted to make a good impression on Mark Fisk, so we got up especially early, dressed in our best outfits, and headed for Lansing to claim the so-important voter files. Road repair around the offsite made us half an hour late, and I rushed into the building for our appointment in a state of panic, sure that my chance to make a good impression had been destroyed. Later, I realized that nobody in Lansing is ever on time for anything and the roads are always under construction. But on that day I was still a Muskegon lady, on Muskegon time, and I apologized to Mark Fisk profusely.

Mark is a short, dark-eyed, intense man. After working with him for eight years and through three campaigns, I can say without hesitation that he is the smartest politician I know. He probably thought I was some kind of a nut, rushing into his office and asking for the voter files. Mark was more accustomed to having potential candidates ask his advice on possibility of running for a state office. Me, I just wanted the voter file.

Eventually, Mark became a good friend and trusted mentor, and the offsite became a second home. One thing Mark was clear about from the beginning was the importance of knocking on doors to talk with voters. He said it over and over again. He looked at Phil and said it. He looked at me and said it. He wouldn't stop saying it.

Finally, I asked him outright, "Is there something about

me that makes you think I'm not willing to knock on doors?"

"No," he replied, "but plenty of people come in here wanting to run for office, and very few of them actually do the work of knocking on doors. You cannot win without committing to that part of the campaign."

I took his advice to heart and thanked him, and he gave me some homework for the next few weeks. "Meet with all of the Democratic elected officials and leaders in your county," he told me. "Talk to them about your interest in running. Then let's meet again."

Before we left, he had one more piece of advice: "Be sure to send each person you meet a thank you note." And I told him I would.

The next week I met with the county treasurer, Tony Moulatsiotis. I met the Democratic state representative in the 92nd district, Doug Bennett, at the Hearthstone Restaurant in Muskegon. I met with Nancy Frye, the previous candidate for the district I would be running in, at her beautiful home on Blue Lake. I had breakfast at the local Bob Evans with Julie Dennis, former state representative in the 92nd district and at that time a candidate for State Senate. I talked with Democratic Party Chair Gary Conrad. My friend Flo (activist Flo Shriver) put me in touch with labor leaders. I met with Walt Christopherson, who at that time was with the International Brotherhood of Electrical Workers (IBEW); John DeWolf of United Auto Workers (UAW); Linda Myers of the Michigan Education Association (MEA); and Steve Kegolovitz, tireless advocate of working families. The list of labor union initials was long and dizzying, and I thought I'd never get them straight: IBEW, UAW, MEA, UFCW, SEIU, AFT, AFSCME. They roll off my tongue now, like the special education acronyms that sprinkled my vocabulary when I was a speech pathologist in the public schools.

I sent out a thank you note after each meeting.

No one discouraged me. But looking back, I wonder if they were all thinking: *Isn't she sweet, she thinks she can actually unseat David Farhat. I'm not going to be the one to tell her it's impossible.*

One brave person said exactly that to me—the then-sheriff, who was running for reelection at the time, George Jurkas. I'll never forget his words. A group of Democrats was standing outside the CIO Hall in downtown Muskegon on a hot July evening, waiting for our monthly meeting to begin, and I found myself standing beside George. Looking me in the eye, he said, "You know you can't win, don't you? You're a sacrificial lamb."

His words had an interesting effect on me. They made me determined to prove him wrong. I discovered later that he was a friend and supporter of Nancy Frye, the woman who had lost the seat I would be running for to David Farhat—not once but twice. So I completely understand where George was coming from when he said this. If Nancy Frye, topnotch professional and well-known politician, couldn't defeat David Farhat, how could I, a complete unknown with no campaign experience or name recognition, even think of defeating a now two-term incumbent? Impossible. Outrageous.

Everyone was still convinced no one could beat a Farhat in Muskegon County.

You've heard the saying, "Ignorance is bliss." There's truth in it. Sometimes it's better to be ignorant of the odds. This was one of those times. The prevailing sense that Farhat was unbeatable no longer discouraged me. Instead, it made me determined to work harder and go farther.

One morning, I noticed the words my daughter Robin had scrawled across her bathroom mirror in red lipstick: *Impossible takes a week.* She likes to occasionally post inspirational messages for herself, but this one seemed perfectly aimed at me.

It was time to attend to some of the more mundane matters of running an election. I picked a campaign name—"Friends of Mary Valentine"—filed the necessary paperwork with the state, and opened a campaign bank account and a post office box. I knew I'd need a photo of myself, which turned into a bit of a problem. I am ridiculously unphotogenic yet vain at the same time—an unfortunate combination. I nearly gave up on the whole idea of running for office after several bad attempts at a campaign portrait. I did finally find a shot with which I was comfortable, and which we used on our first piece of campaign literature—a long pink card with my picture at the top and my qualifications and platform beneath.

Ironically, before the campaign was done, terribly unflattering pictures of me were flashed repeatedly on TV ads across the state and jammed into the mailboxes of thousands of voters. I had to let go of my vanity and realize that there were worse things in the world than unattractive photos of myself. After I became a state representative, every day was picture day. Some pictures were flattering, some were awful, and I just learned to live with it.

Once, during my second term, Kathy Angerer, the majority floor leader, was in the midst of a tumultuous event in the House chamber when a photographer from the *Lansing Journal* snapped her picture while her mouth was unnaturally wide open. A terrible picture of a beautiful woman, it was printed on the front page of the *Lansing Journal*, which I am sure was unpleasant for her. But this same woman passed significant legislation for families of autistic children. From this, I learned that some accomplishments are well worth the price of an unflattering photograph.

In October 2005, I signed up for a training session that Nancy Waters, a longtime Democrat who later became the Muskegon county clerk, had recommended to me. I attended the two-day session run by EMILY's List at the Radisson Hotel in downtown Lansing.[3]

The training and encouragement I received from EMILY's List was invaluable, both in the early days of my campaign and long afterward. We learned how to develop a campaign plan by noting on a calendar the days we would dedicate to knocking on doors and those we would dedicate to parades, debates, and forums. Participants learned how to raise money, develop campaign literature, and formulate strong, concise messages.

I attended other sessions, more training. The Justice Caucus of the Democratic Party has the mission to build a strong and fair Supreme Court, which Michigan desperately needs. They recruit and train progressive candidates. Their one-day training session, Camp Millie, is named after long-time social justice warrior, Millie Jeffries.[4] They present the camp in various places around the state; the one I attended was at the Yacht Club in Holland, Michigan. My fundraising and door-knocking skills were further honed at this topnotch training session.

By late summer, 2005, I was ready to follow Mark Fisk's

---

[3] EMILY's List is an organization that formed after Clarence Thomas was appointed to the Supreme Court despite allegations of sexual harassment by a highly respected professor of law, Anita Hill. The incident made it clear to numerous women voters that being underrepresented in the legislature had a negative impact on their rights and freedoms. The organization that formed as a result had a clear purpose—to encourage and finance women who sought to run for office. The acronym EMILY stands for Early Money Is Like Yeast, meaning that early investments in a campaign would make "dough" rise.

[4] Millie Jeffries was an activist who began as a labor organizer and went on to march with Martin Luther King in the 60's. She worked her entire life to ensure fairness for workers, minorities, and women. In 2000, she even received the highest civilian award that can be bestowed upon a U.S. citizen, the Presidential Medal of Freedom, from Bill Clinton.

advice and try my hand at knocking on doors in my own neighborhood. I had a petition for my run for office, and I'd also created a stack of unprofessional-looking business cards with my name and phone number. The cards, incidentally, were pink—I thought making them valentine-pink was the way to go.[5]

I'll never forget those early outings in my neighborhood. I was equal parts fearful and determined. I would march up to a door, knock, wait for a response, and then, when I was face to face with the resident, eagerly explain what I was doing.

One woman asked whom I would be running against. "David Farhat," I told her. She called her husband to the door.

"Honey, she says she's running against David Farhat!"

"We're both Republicans," they explained, "but we will sign your petition."

When I asked them why, they wouldn't say. But they warmly wished me the best of luck.

A variation on this theme would be repeated throughout the campaign. I began to get a sense that plenty of support existed for my challenge to David Farhat's seat, even among Republican voters. Mostly, though, people asked for anonymity. One woman told me that she feared that openly supporting me could "hurt her son-in-law's business."

I learned from my neighborhood campaigning that many people were aware of Farhat's influence in the community and were intimidated by it. I heard lots of stories while canvassing door-to-door. It's hard to know which stories were

---

[5] Later in the campaign, this decision led to some controversy when my daughter, Robin, and our campaign manager, Chris Kilgroe, decided that playing up my name in this way would marginalize me and distract voters from the serious issues facing our state. Robin and Chris won. Our colors were changed to blue and white.

true and which were untrue, but there was definitely a quietly bad vibe about my adversary. Maybe, I thought, the fact that everyone knew David Farhat was not the advantage for him that people thought it was.

A few stories about Farhat appeared in the *Muskegon Chronicle* before the end of the campaign: one, that he was being sued for trying to cheat the widow of a famous war hero out of her money, and another, that he was being sued for tax issues. Both stories made the front page of the *Chronicle*.

Ironically, Farhat had won his two previous elections running on "family values." And during my campaign, he stayed on message about being the right choice if you cared about family. Yet he was not married and had no children, whereas I have been married to my husband since 1979 and have two children.

I have worked in the schools and devoted my career to helping children. Yet throughout the course of the campaign, my opponent constantly portrayed me as "anti-family." Of course, this sort of hypocrisy has become the norm in political campaigns across the country. In my 2006 run, I certainly received my share of it.

Fortunately, for that particular race, the voters didn't buy it.

I had to do one more thing before I was ready for an all-out run. I signed up for Toastmasters, with the goal of finally getting over my fear of public speaking. I knew there would be no room for my usual panic about addressing a crowd. Toastmasters worked for me, albeit gradually. Slowly and with practice, I became more confident about giving speeches. Today, outside of a few weak butterflies in my tummy before speaking in public, I'm fine. Better than fine—I actually have learned to love standing at a microphone and speaking my mind to an audience.

It was Mike Blake, my campaign organizer (who eventually left Michigan to work for the 2008 Obama campaign), who first taught me how to "glad-hand"—a technique for connecting with voters every bit as important as canvassing and public speaking. Mike was young, ambitious, and smart as a whip. In September 2006, right after the local Labor Day parade at Margaret Drake Elliot Park, Mike gave me my first lesson in glad-handing.

He stood by my side as I walked up to the nearest complete stranger and introduced myself. Part of me felt like it was rude to do that, but Mike was silently pushing me on. The man I approached wasn't upset at being interrupted, so

Jeff Rector, Deputy Campaign Manager, Eric Samuelson, Emily's List Volunteer, Loyce Tapken, longtime Muskegon activist, Chris Kilgroe, campaign manager, and Mike Blake, caucus organizer who went on to work for President Obama.

after this first attempt (and with more prompting), I tried again. I approached another person, an older woman this time, and told her I was Mary Valentine, running for state representative of the 91st district. I shook her hand.

After a few more shaky approaches, the training wheels came off. I was in a groove, thanks to Mike's support and patience. I'll always be grateful to Mike for his guidance that day—the day I became a better campaigner. Mike went on to secure a job in D.C. with the Obama Administration, and I still see him from time to time—once when he came back to Michigan to campaign for President Obama and once when Phil and I were invited for a tour of the White House. I value his friendship, then and now.[6]

My nephew, Brad Anderson, also gave me some great suggestions on how to work a room while campaigning, which he had picked up as a successful businessman. Probably the best tip he gave me was to discreetly look out of the corner of my eye as I was nearing the end of a conversation to pinpoint the person I would like to talk to next.

"When that person is free," he told me, "politely excuse yourself from the conversation you are in and make your move." I used this trick constantly. Worked like a charm.

I also remember being at an event at the Maritime Museum in Muskegon and getting an early lesson in putting myself out there from two dedicated Democrats—Gary Conrad, then chair of the Democratic Party, and Lou Ann Voss. Sitting at one of the round tables, we were waiting for the event to begin and chatting while people wandered in and found their seats.

"Mary, you better get out there and shake some hands," Lou Ann said.

"That's right," echoed Gary.

Initially, I was timid and afraid to interrupt people, but I soon discovered people didn't mind and were happy to talk with me. It got easier. My shyness faded. My public-speaking anxiety all but disappeared, and my willingness to approach a stranger grew stronger. After all, I had a purpose and a

---

[6] Mike is now running for the State Assembly in New York: Bronx, District 79

message—and all I wanted was a chance to serve.

Another important tip was one I received from Julie Dennis, who had been the state representative in the 92nd District and was running for state senate during my first campaign.

I was at the Roosevelt Park Day Parade, walking down the middle of the street waving to people, as I had seen Senator Gerald Van Woerkom do.

"Mary, you need to run from side to side, shaking hands," she insisted. From then on, I covered three times the territory of anyone else in the parade—running from one side of the road to the other, shaking hands, high-fiving kids, and sharing pleasantries. Parades were exhausting, but I loved every minute of them.

Slowly, my political identity became as much a part of who I really am as my brown eyes.

Chapter V

The Cast of Characters

It's Christmas Eve of 2010. I should be focusing on our Valentine family Christmas traditions. But my campaign defeat is still fresh, and I'm still grieving. I find myself thinking about my two terms and all it meant to me to be the state representative for my district. I worked so hard. I accomplished so much. It's hard to face the fact that none of it mattered enough to voters to give me a chance to represent them in the Senate.

My thoughts drift back to a cold February night after a long day in session during my first term. Driving to Newago County from Lansing, I find myself alone on a dark road, double-checking a scrap of paper with scribbled directions to the VFW Hall. In my pre-GPS-driving days, these directions are my lifeline. I don't really know where I am, but hope I'm heading to the hall. There is nothing but farmland around me, and I start to wonder if I've taken a wrong turn. Suddenly, the VFW Hall is in front of me, its parking lot full. Parking, I take a few deep relieved breaths and enter. Eight legislators were invited to this meeting about protecting water resources in West Michigan. I'm the only one to show up.

During my years in the legislature, this happened again and again. Republicans just didn't show up to these tough meetings. Of course, holding open meetings with people who don't agree with you is hard. I should know. I struggled through meetings with realtors and farmers—even though they pretty much think Democrats are three-horned baby-killers who raise taxes for the sole purpose of destroying their businesses. But hey, attending tough meetings is our job. It's what we were elected for and paid to do.

For instance, Melissa Smith, a candidate for the Holton School Board at the time, set up a Town Hall meeting to discuss Holton's school budget mess. Instead of complaining, as everyone does, about school funding, Melissa took action— she participated in our democracy and organized a forum, personally inviting legislators. Many of us agreed to come to the event, listen to concerns, and answer questions. On the night of that meeting, I was again the only one who bothered to show up. In front of roughly 150 people, on a stage at the Whitehall High School auditorium, I answered questions as honestly as I could for an hour and a half. The questions came from parents, teachers, and students who were concerned about their schools and education policy. Goeff Hansen, who is our current state senator and was a state representative at the time, failed to show up. I was upset about this lack of respect for voters then, and I'm still upset about it today—not because it was tough to do it alone (it was actually easier because I didn't have to continually counter their misinformation) but because of the disrespect it shows for constituents. It was a bad reflection on all of us. What message does it send that representatives in Lansing care so little about their constituents' struggles? And why aren't voters more up in arms about it?

Another memory: this one concerning a group of Oakridge students who made the trip from Muskegon to Lansing to advocate for something they believed in—the Michigan Promise, a scholarship given to any Michigan student who achieved good test scores. Bob Wood, a political science teacher in the Oakridge School District, taught his high school students how to advocate for the issues they cared about. Bob is a wise teacher and knows students learn far more about political science by taking action than they ever could learn from a textbook. Because his students don't necessarily come from homes that can afford to send their children to college, the issue of continuing to grant worthy students the Michigan Promise Scholarship was important, and students had worked diligently to get the test scores they needed to earn it. Politicians had then yanked it away from them before they could benefit from it.

So the students came to the capital advocating for continued funding for the scholarship. The kids were well prepared. They knew all the details of the program and could explain why it was still a good idea for Michigan, and they had circulated petitions to present to the leaders of the state. After I introduced them to Governor Jennifer Granholm, they gave her the petitions and expressed their hopes that the scholarship would continue. If their parents could have seen how brave and articulate they were on that day, they would have been so proud! I was happy to have invited those young people to take part in their democracy.

The staff of Republican Senator Gerald VanWoerkom, on the other hand, called the school to complain about the students. Later, this same elected senator made the kids feel brushed off, making them wait an hour before he would talk with them without any explanation.

The House Republican leader, Kevin Elsenheimer, was even worse. "You just have to work hard, like I did," he told the Oakridge students. Elsenheimer was addressing a group of young people who had faced financial and family struggles beyond anything he could imagine. I'm happy to report that his condescending attitude didn't discourage these young people; it strengthened their resolve.

I know that life isn't fair, that bad things happen to good people. I know that in politics, perception is reality. Still, at this point in my recovery, as I sit writing and remembering, I wonder why all my commitment and concern for the people of my district didn't translate into votes.

I know that, in time, this won't bother me. But today, it still does.

* * * *

I decided in the summer of 2005 that I needed a kitchen cabinet, because Grey's *Guide to running a Successful Campaign* recommended it. But how does one create a cabinet?

During the election cycle that led to my campaign, I'd met a man named George Crosby. Retired and new to Muskegon, I'd seen him throw himself into Howard Dean's 2004 political campaign with great passion. When he introduced me to his friend Chris Kilgroe, an equally passionate activist, a strong political friendship resulted.

I soon learned that Chris was a natural leader and organizer with excellent political instincts. I definitely wanted his help, if he would agree. Chris was the one who initially asked me to run for this office and supported me in making that decision. So he was the first person I formally asked to become part of my cabinet. He jumped at the chance.

No one worked harder for me than Chris. Truly, he deserves much of the credit for our two victories. His political wisdom and his work ethic kept me going, through good times and bad. He pushed me to try new tactics and encouraged me when things looked grim. Everyone running for office needs a Chris Kilgroe in his or her corner.

Another friend I chose early for the cabinet was Ginger Graham, a woman I had first met back in 2004 at the showing of the film *The Truth About the Iraqi War* at the Unitarian Universalist Congregation in Muskegon. That night, I met a woman who was as fed up as I was with an unnecessary war and tax cuts for the wealthy. Plus she was bright, enthusiastic, and willing to work hard for something she believed in. She was the second person I approached, and like Chris, she jumped in.

Now we had three people at the table.

Soon afterward, I attended a potluck where I met Chris Bedford, a filmmaker and political organizer. Chris was one of the founders of the Sweetwater Market, a local organic farmer's market; he and his partner, Diana Jancek, had been community activists for some time. Chris was a master wordsmith and a keen advisor, and quickly became invaluable to our cabinet. Continuing to advise me while I was serving, he contributed two essential elements: He kept me informed about agricultural issues in the state, and he could always make me laugh.

The next cabinet member was my own brother, Doug Hostetler, who has shared my values and political beliefs for many years. He had been politically active in the 91st District even before my campaign, so he was an obvious choice to become part of the team. Doug is a natural leader and an excellent writer, two necessary attributes for any successful campaign. He also became our designated "sign guy," putting out signs and repairing them so they would hold out against the wind in a windy city.

Doug's wife, Judy, worked with Phil to prepare the financial reports that were due several times a year. These reports, in a fierce campaign like ours, are critical. Both sides comb through them for anything they can use against their opponent, which creates a good deal of stress for those preparing the reports. In a grassroots campaign like ours, we depended on hundreds of small donors to fund the campaign. Between having to account for every penny we received and spent, this was an incredibly demanding and stressful job.

Others joined me early on, including a young woman I'd met during the Kerry campaign, Jennifer Geno, who lived only a few blocks away. Jennifer is chock full of good ideas, as sensible as a wool hat, and knows how to fully commit to a cause she believes in.[7]

And there was my daughter, who was 24 years old at the time. Robin had caught the political bug during the Kerry campaign and I knew she would be an asset to mine. She is a people person with astute political instincts and a wonderful sense of humor—something we came to depend on as the campaign unfolded. Plus, I loved having her near me during my effort—having her be part of the adventure was one of the best things about running for office.

My burly son, Shawn, helped out where he could— particularly with creating messages, at which he excels. Democrats are foolish to not enlist him in that job to this day. Later, he helped construct, put up, and take down our signs.

And though my husband was not literally sitting at the table, his work with the financials made the whole thing possible. The texture of his life, after I started running for office, changed completely. Trips to the post office to pick up checks and to the bank to deposit them dominated his days, not to mention recording those checks, keeping the books, and creating the reports.

---

[7] Since those days Jennifer and her husband, Josh, have become parents to two darling little girls, Gabi and Lydia.

Finally, I invited a longtime friend, Cynthia George, whom I had met years earlier when our pre-teen daughters had become close friends in the sixth grade. Both our girls could be mischief-makers at times during their teen years—which created a strong bond between us two moms. I wanted that bond to be part of the network of supporters in the cabinet. I asked. She agreed.

A group of activists and organizers with varying degrees of experience in the political realm, we had unmatched passion and commitment. We were also determined to win. The fact that we weren't sure how to begin did not stop, or even discourage, us.

In August 2005, we began meeting around the round oak table in my kitchen for a few months, until the Democratic leaders in Lansing deemed us a targeted race and put resources into our campaign. By that time, our fundraising operation, which I will discuss later, had also raised enough money to hire a staff.

Every Wednesday night at 7:00 p.m., the cabinet gathered in my kitchen, munching on chips and popcorn, drinking coffee or soda. Slowly, we hammered out an initial strategy. First, we evaluated the strengths and weaknesses of both David Farhat and yours truly. We tried to match my strengths with his weaknesses to develop a message. We also strategized ways to improve what we felt were my areas of weakness, chiefly inexperience in government and business and lack of name recognition.

We taped two huge pieces of paper to the wall—one for David Farhat and one for me—listing strengths and weaknesses, with the goal of creating a strong contrast between the two candidates. This session wasn't easy for me—having people who know me best shout out my weaknesses toughened me up for what was to come. For example: "David

Farhat is a successful businessman, an area where Mary is inexperienced."

They were right about that. Although I was from a family of entrepreneurs—my parents and all of my siblings owned successful businesses—I had focused on the area of education.

"David Farhat has strong name recognition. Mary is a complete unknown."

But we all knew I was the better candidate with serious strengths: "Mary knows about the public education system and cares about education. David Farhat doesn't."

"David Farhat has a questionable reputation; some people say he can't be trusted. Mary Valentine is a Sunday School Teacher."

We wrote all these statements on paper taped to the wall. The whole session was incredibly clarifying and reinforcing, helping us see the challenge that lay ahead of us. That, along with some prompting from long-time Democrat and former prosecutor Paul Ladas, is how we came up with our campaign slogan: "Mary Valentine, someone you can trust."

We used it on our first "lit piece" (political lingo for campaign literature). Eventually we had it printed on tee shirts and banners. It was an effective slogan; we never felt the need to change it.

Our next challenge was to create and organize our first real fundraiser. Chris Bedford set it up at the home of Celia Said, on the outskirts of Montague near the shores of Lake Michigan. Ginger made the invitations, dated for the first day of October 2005. We made up a list of people we knew and had an envelope-addressing party. The cabinet hand-addressed 300 envelopes, all the while laughing, chatting, and talking politics.

My nephew Brad, owner of a grocery store in Glen Arbor,

supplied wine. Several people brought food—finger food, casseroles, and salads. Marcia Hovey-Wright, an old pro with fundraisers, advised us on how to keep the event professional. Marcia had just run a campaign for state representative in the 92nd district the previous summer and was the experienced one. She was fighting cancer at that time, so I wasn't sure if I should ask for her help. But she was so generous. A remarkable woman, since that time she has not only fully recovered, but has gone on to become the state representative in the 92nd District.

My friend and fellow teacher Cindy Adam's husband, John Adams, a high school teacher and part of a trio of musicians that also included another friend from my speech pathologist days—Pete Bennett—provided music. So not only did we have a fabulous site for our event—a house overlooking Lake Michigan—and great food, we had wonderful live music as well. My friends Carol and Greg Schwemin posted a series of signs directing people to the home of Celia Said. My son, Shawn, and his buddy Michael Dean handled the "Valentine Shuttle," parking peoples' cars at Medford Park and providing a ride to Celia's home and back to their cars after the event. We asked for a donation of $25 per person, which seemed like an outrageous amount to me at the time. Many gave much more than that.

The turnout was fantastic.

Because it was the first fundraiser, it was my first stump speech. My sister Maggie Hostetler was there, along with her longtime partner, Lorri Sipes. My mom also was there, as well as many old and new friends, colleagues, and political allies. Our hostess, Celia Said, spoke a few words of welcome, and Chris Kilgroe introduced me. It was time for me to give a rousing speech about my beliefs and goals. I was, as you can imagine, terrified.

But Chris had helped me prepare. He had advised me to put my ideas into coherent order and repeat them, practicing aloud until I could recite the speech without notes. Despite my long-time fear of public speaking, the speech went well, in part because the crowd was fabulous. They clapped enthusiastically at all the right places, laughed at my jokes, and burst into wild applause as I finished. It was a great party and when it was over, we had brought in $5,000.

We had more fundraisers, and putting them together got easier as we learned what worked and what didn't. My Muskegon friends Doug and Rose Jolman, along with Dan and Jane Horton, all hosted wonderful events in their homes on my behalf.

Then, on Valentine's Day of 2006, we had a huge fundraiser that effectively launched my campaign in style. It was at the Polish Union Hall on Henry Street in Norton Shores; the attendees included many people I had never even met before. Money flowed in, the place was packed and noisy, and we even had to run out for extra food. Sharon Polidan provided the entertainment with her beautiful singing voice. When it was time for me to speak, Chris, as usual, introduced me. I knew this speech would be harder—so many people were waiting to hear what I had to say. Heart racing and palms sweating, I started speaking through my nervousness, talking about fear and hope (yes, I articulated those concepts even before Obama did!) The crowd loved it. The night was another huge success. I invited Sharon to join my cabinet. Afterwards, no local Democrat ever again said I couldn't win this race.

Something else happened as well—an internal shift. I began to feel like a state representative.

My kitchen cabinet helped me make the all-important announcement of my candidacy. As a group, we searched the

Muskegon area for the right spot for the event. After much driving and discussion, we chose the site of the old Saapi Paper Mill. We sent word of the event to our supporters, wanting a strong showing. Dan Farrough, the Democratic House press secretary, came over from Lansing and helped me rehearse for questions from the media. I wanted to be expertly prepared, but I needn't have worried; no press showed up for the event. Still, it went beautifully—perfect weather, dozens of supporters, positive energy, and posters galore. Children waved flags and Valentine-themed pink posters.

We decided to take some pictures at the site to be used later in the campaign. I stood in front of the mill with my cabinet and my supporters *behind* me, which was disconcerting, but I wanted to be photographed with them at my back as I announced my candidacy. It was enormously gratifying to have them near me. I felt both supported and humbled.

It was now official: *Mary Valentine for State Representative. Someone You Can Trust.*

Chapter VI

Our Mantra

I'm at my usual table with my Acer Netbook, my coffee, and my orange cranberry muffin.

I'm recovering from the task of writing thank-you notes— 700 of them, to be exact—earlier in the week. My right hand is still sore, but I'm not complaining. Supporters not only gave generously from their wallets, they gave generously of their hearts and their time. Their generosity and faith in me has me feeling guilty this morning about losing the Senate seat. Although I know it's pointless to feel this way, sometimes I do. I'm hopeful that, in time, the guilt about losing will fade.

I'm frustrated by the plethora of new lies that stream out of the mouths of some of my Republican colleagues. Just this morning on MLive.com, an online news source, someone stated again that while in office, Governor Jennifer Granholm had increased the budget from $32 billion to $47 billion. There isn't one ounce of truth to that statement—and the Republicans know it. The extra $15 billion in the equation is pass-through money: funds that came from the federal government and were passed along to state programs. The only thing Governor Granholm possibly could have done to avoid this was send it back to the Feds. With the huge budget shortfall in this state, that would have been a big help, now, wouldn't it?

Republican leaders trumpeted that lie for the entire time

Jennifer Granholm was governor of Michigan. Now, two years into the term of Rick Snyder, our new Republican governor, the budget has increased by another $4 billion. Funny thing, though—they never mention it any more.

Sadly, I can hear my Republican friends—good citizens, heartfelt people—complaining about my tendency to hold government leaders accountable for what they say. My Republican friends get angry with me for simply demanding the truth, but I have a special interest in truth in politics. Because just as the State Republican Party lied about Governor Granholm and the budget increase, they lied about me.

* * * *

By the spring of 2006, my civilian life had disappeared. I retired from my job as a speech pathologist in May to concentrate more fully on fundraising. I had less time to share with friends and family. I was (and still am) exceedingly fortunate to be married to Phil Valentine, who picked up the household duties I no longer had time for. He grocery-shopped, kept up with the laundry, and prepared meals. He was the foundation of our team as we moved forward.

My staff knew that the Farhat campaign would push back hard as the strength of my campaign grew. Battles were coming, and the team wanted to be as proactive as possible. The most important strategy for standing up to political attacks was to talk to as many voters as possible before the campaigns went into high gear. So we did exactly that. We went from neighborhood to neighborhood in the 91st district, knocking on doors and speaking directly to the voters. Our thinking was that once people saw me and talked to me, they would be less likely to believe that I had ties to Iraqi terrorists, or that I was an extremist on social issues, or that I was cruel or dangerous.

It was a good strategy, because these were some of the actual accusations that were thrown at me in the fall as the campaign went into high gear.

Yes, I knocked on doors every day. I talked to voters every day. I met the people of my district and asked them about the issues important to them. And I listened.

I worked side by side with my wonderful volunteers. We went to wealthy suburban neighborhoods and we went down dusty country roads. We canvassed on suburban streets, in trailer parks, at condo units, and at homes on Lake Michigan. We knocked in every kind of weather, including rain and snow.

Doors: the mantra of our campaign.

Our first target for canvassing (in September 2005) was Roosevelt Park, the community abutting mine—one square mile of residential neighborhoods. It was dense with a good Democratic base, so the canvassing was encouraging. I was still a speech pathologist in the Reeths-Puffer Schools that September. Every day after work, I stopped and knocked on doors for a few hours. On Saturdays, Phil and I went out together to some of the more rural areas. He drove; I knocked on doors. I even went out alone for a couple of hours on Sunday nights.

We targeted registered voters using the information from the voter file I had sought earlier in the year from Mark Fisk. At this point in the campaign, pretty much everybody thought I had an impossible task in front of me. I ignored this belief and faithfully knocked on doors and talked to voters. I reported the growing number of doors on which I had knocked to every Democratic group I talked to.

As soon as it got too cold to canvass, my team gave me lists of voters to call on the phone. First I would send a card with my picture on it to each targeted home in the precinct, telling them I would be calling. Then I called, after which I sent out another card: either "nice talking to you" or "sorry I missed you." I sometimes even wrote little notes on them about what we had discussed. All together that winter, I made 4,000 phone calls to voters. My family spent evenings stamping and addressing the pre- and postcards while we watched TV.

When spring rolled around, I began knocking on doors again, along with the many friends and volunteers who had joined the effort. During the summer months, we developed a routine. We started at roughly 2:00 in the afternoon and went out in teams of two to four people. After a few hours of knocking, we'd connect via cell phone and decide on a place to meet for dinner. We were always eager to see one another and swap stories about the people we'd met and spoken to. Then we went out again until it got dark.

I did this with my volunteers from May through October 2006.

I'm still so grateful to the volunteers who canvassed with me. It isn't easy to knock on the door of a complete stranger and talk with him or her about a candidate. But we all got better at it. The best doorknocker on the team was Chris. His long legs covered territory far more quickly than any of the rest of us. He went out tirelessly to talk with voters about me.

Some volunteers drove their own cars. Mostly, though, during the first campaign, we drove my big white Pontiac mini-van, which had one interesting distinguishing feature: the wipers were stuck in the up position. We slapped on some Mary Valentine signs and called it our "Valentine-mobile." It tore down city streets and country roads and pulled in and out of driveways day after day, week after week. By the end of the campaign, the van was shot and I replaced it with the red Chevy Vibe.

An election win began to look less and less impossible. Yet we kept getting word that the lobby corps in Lansing wasn't taking us seriously. I was too much of a complete unknown in Lansing, where David Farhat's family had a lobbying firm and a history in Michigan politics. I still got an occasional earful about how no one could defeat a Farhat in Muskegon County. At the same time, we started getting increasingly colorful comments from the voters we visited— uncensored opinions about my opponent.

To buoy us up over the long months, we started writing down the best comments and even competed for the funniest "quote of the day."

A couple of winners:

"I'd vote for Kruschev before I'd vote for Farhat again."

"I wouldn't vote for him for dogcatcher."

A pattern emerged. David Farhat, a charming and char-ismatic guy, was incredibly gifted at gaining peoples' trust. But he also had developed a reputation for taking advantage of people. He apparently had reneged on his end of the bargain in too many situations. We spoke to a surprising number of angry people who were thrilled to support me.[8]

And I was thrilled to receive their support. In fact, I loved canvassing. I saw so many different homes and neighbor-hoods and met such fascinating people. For the most part, I felt safe. But one thing I learned early on is that the people of the 91st district love their dogs.

I'm a dog lover, and I never minded hearing a dog barking in the yards or behind the doors I was knocking on. I espe-

---

[8] All this negativity must have been tough for David Farhat to endure. I hope it altered his life for the better. I would like to think that campaign changed the way he did things.

cially loved the ones that would bark ferociously while wagging their tails. Often, after I took a step forward, the dog would retreat and continue barking. By the end, the pooch would be hiding behind a tree or bush, still barking non-stop. It was hard to take them seriously.

One home I went to in Fruitport, though, still makes my heart pound in fear when I think about it. The house was off the road a bit and up a small hill. Right next to the walkway to the house was a fenced-in area that held six adult German Shepherds, all of them barking, snarling, and baring their teeth. They were locked up, so I kept going, inching my way closer to the house. When I got to the door, I realized there were two more snarling dogs inside the house. I tucked the lit piece in the door and ran to my car, never to return to that house again.

Another time, two gigantic Great Danes ran up to the door and then surprised me by running straight through the door! The "door" turned out to be merely a hanging screen. They completely cornered me before I realized the most danger I faced was getting licked to death. Meanwhile, Chris, my driver for the day, jumped out of the car and ran to rescue me.

One August day during the second campaign, Anne Pawli and I were out in my Vibe, knocking on doors on Sherman Boulevard. After we pulled into a driveway, I hopped out of the car and walked across the yard to get to the door. Suddenly a pit-bull/rotweiller charged me and took a big chunk out of my leg. Blood gushed and ran down my leg. The apologetic homeowner came out and gave me her phone number. Anne took me right to Hackley Hospital, where we checked in.

"It's Mary Valentine," I heard someone whisper.

Once I was in the examination room, a doctor popped in

his head and said, "I see we have someone famous here today."

I just smiled.

Next came a nurse who apparently didn't know me.

"How did you happen to be walking to the house?" she asked.

"I am running for office and was out campaigning."

"Which party?"

"Democratic."

"Oh, I'm a Republican."

I repeated the story all over again when the police officer came in to take a report. He, too, told me he was a Republican. I couldn't resist mentioning that a police organization had just endorsed me, which clearly didn't impress him. I'm happy to report that those two Republicans were extremely professional and gave me great care. I changed the dressing for a few weeks and recovered completely. It was my only dog bite on the campaign trail.

During the first campaign, few people had ever heard of me, so getting my name out to the voting public was critical. That was why we sent out the pre-cards to let people know I would be stopping by. One day, I knocked on the door of a Whitehall teacher shortly after she had received my pre-card—a few minutes after, in fact. She obviously was stunned to see me at the door. I'm pretty sure she told all her friends that story, which got my name out even more.

Today people still tell me they remember seeing me at their doorsteps and still remember our conversations. It was incredibly time-consuming, but I enjoyed meeting so many wonderful people and having so many stimulating conversations. Sure, there were a few sourpusses, but overwhelmingly, people were good to me. And I learned about the struggles people face and the issues that are important to them.

One experience was particularly touching. After graduating from high school, my son, Shawn, became a caregiver for a while, providing assistance to patients who were nearing the end of their lives and needed care their families weren't always able to provide. It was the perfect job for him; he is strong enough to lift and carry people, but also incredibly gentle. His first client was a man known only to us as Bill. Shawn was always talking to us about Bill and telling various stories about him. They had become friends and he was clearly attached to Bill.

One day, a team of three—Chris Kilgroe, Jeff Rector, and me—were knocking on doors on Windflower Way in a subdivision south of Pontaluna Road, when Chris came running up to me. "Bill Langlois is dying," he said breathlessly, "but his wife, Ginny, wants to meet you. Let's go quickly."

It seems that Chris had knocked on the door of my son's client, who was in his final hours. When Chris realized this, he offered to leave, but Bill's wife, Ginny, asked Chris if he was canvassing for Mary Valentine. When Chris answered yes, Ginny Langlois insisted that I come over so she could meet me.

At first, Chris and Jeff suggested they wait outside, but Ginny would have none of that. She insisted we all come up to the house, so she could talk with us. She wanted to tell me personally how highly she thought of my son. At such a difficult and deeply emotional time, she wanted to meet my team and me. I learned that the man my son always talked about was in fact the owner of a local furniture store. His precious wife, Ginny, was such an angel on that day, I'm surprised she didn't sprout wings. I was touched beyond measure; we all were. We left the Langlois home in silence, moved beyond words.

Knocking on doors was a way to get to know the physical

aspects of my district as well—the working-class neighbor-hoods, the condos by the lake, the trailer parks where people were struggling, and the swankier mobile home parks. We met wealthy folks with deep concern for their fellow human beings and other wealthy folks who seemed to care only about their own pocketbooks.

I remember one discussion with a man who was deeply concerned about "overpriced" teachers' insurance, a myth perpetuated by the Mackinac Center, a right-wing propaganda machine. This man lived in a gigantic house on Mona Lake, so I couldn't figure out why the cost of insurance for teachers was the issue he was most concerned about!

Another man I met canvassing in Mason County during my Senate race lived in an exquisite log home on Hamlin Lake. The home was large with an outside picnic area over-looking the water. He simply couldn't stop talking about how terrible Obama was and got himself quite worked up about it. He was distraught that Obama wanted to end the Bush tax cuts for people with an income higher than $250,000 a year—a salary most of us would long for, even if we had to pay more in taxes. By the end of the conversation, I felt sorry for the guy. He was so worried about losing a piece of his wealth, he couldn't even enjoy what he had. Give me my humble three-bedroom ranch any day.

The moment of approaching a door, knocking, and won-dering who would answer never got old for me. Fifty percent of the time, no one answered, and in that case I left a card saying I was sorry I had missed him or her. The other 50% of the time, people were mostly pleasant, interested in what I had to say, and appreciative of the effort I was making to reach out to voters. Make no mistake; I met a few grouchy people. I don't really blame them—they might have been watching a favorite TV show or napping. I just gave them my biggest smile and a warm greeting, and they almost always came around and entered a brief, civil discussion. Even when we didn't agree, most people were willing to at least talk to me.

I discovered neighborhoods I didn't know existed. One was behind the Norton Shores Public Library off Seminole Street. I canvassed there in the spring of 2006, when the streets were lined with red buds and the magnolia trees in full bloom. A sweet fragrance filled the air. Birds were singing. It was a peaceful retirement neighborhood and on that afternoon, it felt like a fairy wonderland.

One day I knocked on the door of a tarpaper shack. Literally. A house covered with tarpaper, with a nice owner with whom I enjoyed talking. The next day I found myself inside a gigantic mansion on Mona Lake. I truly came face to face with the great financial diversity of my district.

Once, I came upon a family whose possessions were on the front sidewalk. They couldn't find jobs and were in foreclosure, so were selling all their earthly possessions and moving out of state. Talking with this devastated family brought the seriousness of the foreclosure problem into clear focus. I never forgot the sight of this family's belongings on the sidewalk, and the reality of them selling everything they owned so that they could get out of Michigan.

Foreclosure stories became part of my canvassing. In Whitehall, a small lakeside town just north of Muskegon, I had a sad exchange with a schoolteacher who was on the verge of losing his home to foreclosure. Another time, in Egelston Township, I knocked on the door of a man who was days away from losing his home. That time, the conversation was short, because he was so angry. Perhaps in his eyes, my ambition to get into government made me partly responsible for his misfortune.

I talked to a man in Twin Lake who had been trying for years to find gainful employment. Demoralized by his situation, he also expressed anger. I think I convinced him that I was on his side and would work hard in Lansing to solve Michigan's dire economic problems. Before I left, he told me that he appreciated the fact that I had come to his door to talk with him. I wished him good luck.

Behind another door was a man who had been marked as "strong Dem" on my walk sheet, which I realized was a clear mistake shortly after our conversation began. He told me he would never vote for me. "I'm a Republican," he said. "I believe in the American way—make as much money as you can."

I kept quiet, but I was thinking: *Silly me. I thought the American way was about liberty and equality.*

Once, a sweet 11-year-old girl answered the door of a stunningly beautiful home off Henry Street in Norton Shores. When her dad heard my name he yelled from the other room, "Is that Mary Valentine? Tell her to go away! We want nothing to do with the likes of her."

Ouch. I felt worse for the girl, though. She was clearly embarrassed.

An older woman I talked to in the Roodmont area in Norton Shores was distraught over a decision she had to face: whether or not to remain in her own home. She couldn't hear anything political while that weighed on her mind. So I dropped all political talk and just listened to her, instead. Before I left she asked for one of my signs to put in her yard.

Once I talked to a woman who yelled at me for a good five minutes about the job situation, while I stood dumbfounded. When I left, she shouted at me, "I'm voting for you!" Apparently, she was distraught and frustrated, and appreciated the opportunity to get these emotions off her chest.

Another time a man came to the door of his house, thinking that I was a Republican because my party affiliation wasn't mentioned in my campaign literature. The man had been tricked into voting Republican in the past and thought this was just another trick. I nearly got thrown off the porch! In the end, I convinced him that I was really a Democrat and proud of it.

I met one young woman who was living on her own in a trailer park. She was trying to go back to school to become a nurse but couldn't find funding. This was during my second campaign, when I was already serving as a state representative. I went back to the office and combed heaven and earth to find scholarship information to send to her. A few years later, I was at a Service Employees International Union (SEIU) event in Clare, Michigan. She reintroduced herself to me, let me know she was now in training to become a nurse, and thanked me.

It was an extremely gratifying moment.

I remember an afternoon in July 2006, when the temperature and humidity hovered at around 95 degrees. The hot sun beat down on me while I trudged down Brooks Road in Fruitport Township. I began to feel sorry for myself. "What in the world am I doing out here, in this hot, dusty place day after day, when I could be at the lake or home reading a book in my air-conditioned bedroom?" I asked myself.

But I caught myself, remembering the millions of Americans who have died protecting our right to self-governance, including the men and women serving in the military who were making sacrifices overseas that same day—also in withering heat. I was just walking down a hot, dusty road and was in no danger. That put a quick end to my moment of self-pity.

I will always remember knocking on Eric Justian's door. I

soon learned he was an online writer and Web site specialist—though on that day, he was just another potential constituent. His number-one concern was healthcare. He described observing many bright and talented young people, stuck in dead-end jobs, whose dreams were to start their own businesses. Without adequate healthcare coverage for their families, they often lacked the resources to realize this dream. Eric was right—this was a real problem, which, if resolved, could help boost the economy.[9] I didn't have much information, so I gave him an admittedly vague answer, which didn't satisfy him. When I got home that evening, I forwarded further information about this topic to him. I don't remember exactly what I sent him, but I think he was impressed that I took the time to address his concern.

About a year later, when someone was ripping me apart in the comment section of a blog, he responded with the nicest piece about me. "Mary Valentine is not your typical politician," he wrote. He went on to explain the extra effort I had made to communicate with him when I had knocked on his door that day. He described how I had responded to his concerns about healthcare coverage for working families.

Another gratifying moment.

I will say that, generally, the most mean-spirited people I encountered were those who called themselves "pro-life." They slammed doors in my face or hurled rude comments at me during parades. They also were unwilling to enter into any sort of dialogue with me about the issue of legalized abortions. These were die-hard voters who wouldn't vote for a candidate who lacked the endorsement of Michigan Right-to-Life or didn't use their exact terminology. I consider myself "pro-solution" on this issue, which I will discuss in more

---

[9] That problem has since been resolved by the Affordable Care Act.

depth in Chapter XVII.

I can honestly say that at end of a day of knocking on doors and speaking with voters, I was exhausted, but happy. Campaigns can be filled with disagreements, tension, and difficult decisions, but when I was knocking on doors and talking with the citizens of my district, I could leave rhetoric and conflict behind me and talk one-on-one with my constituents about the issues that mattered to them. I loved doing this. I miss it to this day.

But another crucial part of running a campaign was a little more difficult for me—albeit critical to my success. And that part was fundraising.

Chapter VII

Dialing for Dollars

It's a Thursday afternoon in January 2011, and I'm my favorite table at The Coffee House. Although the streets are icy and the world outside is as white as a snow globe, the place is packed. I'm thinking about Elizabeth Kubler Ross's five stages of grief: anger, hurt, denial, bargaining—and finally, acceptance. Kubler Ross wrote that when a person reaches that final stage, he or she is ready to leave the loss behind and move on, stronger for having had the experience. And at this point in my recovery, there is no doubt in my mind that I'm a better person for having made the effort to further serve my country.

Since the race, angry thoughts and second guesses sometimes pop up uninvited. Today, though, neither anger nor regret is rearing its ugly head. They may return tomorrow, but it's nice to have them gone today.

It's a good day. Earlier today, I ran into a few former constituents. They told me they are disappointed that I lost the race and that they were disgusted by the ugliness of the Hansen campaign.

I hear this often, in different settings: the grocery store, the mall. "We miss having you fighting for us in Lansing!"

Such kind words from friends and strangers alike are the precious aftermath of serving the public—as a candidate and later a state representative. Others, who worked just as hard as I did (including my family) don't always get a chance to hear these kind words. But I had a particularly strong bond with activist Democrats—because of the nature of the 91st District, every one of them had to be in my corner for me to win.

Even as our lives move on, taking us in different directions, I still value those friendships.

* * * *

When I first decided to run for office in 2005, I didn't think about all the funds I would need to raise. I was naïve about money in politics, which may have been a good thing. I was able to transform my grassroots campaign into a working political machine without wondering if it was even possible. But I was soon shocked and overwhelmed to discover that the responsibility of raising the necessary funds to run a respectable campaign was pretty much all in my corner.

Every political expert with whom I spoke gave me the same advice: "The best way to raise money is for the candidate herself to call and ask for it."

Call and ask for it. This quickly became the most difficult aspect of running for office. Here's the drill: Find a comfortable place to sit (for hours), refer to your endless call sheets, and proceed to call everyone you know—and a lot of people you don't know—and ask them to give you money. Yup. That's what you have to do. Beg for money every day.

Running for office is expensive. You need yard signs, billboards, posters, flyers, and literature. You need a campaign headquarters with computers, printers, and phones. My campaigns were highly competitive and hard fought. I was running to win, which made the process all the more expensive—I needed regular mailings, printed ads, TV ads, campaign managers, and a working staff. It all cost plenty. And the only way to get the funds was to constantly ask for them.

I grew up in a humble household and my parents felt it was important to teach their five children financial responsibility at a young age. I got my 25-cent allowance on Friday nights and knew better than to ask for more before the next Friday. I was taught to be responsible and hard working, both from experience and from my parents' example.

That is hardly the background one needs to be able to comfortably call people and ask them to give you their hard-earned money for your expensive campaign!

Yes, we held fundraisers, and the fundraisers also brought money in. But when you get right down to it, the only way to keep dollars flowing in is to continue to make those calls—keep calling, keep reminding, keep begging.

I made it a part of my daily routine. Sometimes I'd call from my car. Sometimes I'd sit on the back porch with a big glass of lemonade, feet up, enjoying a view of my flowers while I called. On wet or cold days, I sat in the wicker chair next to my bedroom window with my phone.

After I had a campaign headquarters, I called from the office, where it was harder for me to procrastinate. If my staffers noticed that I was stalling, stopping to make coffee or starting unnecessary conversations, they'd remind me to get back to the phones. They knew all my tricks and my excuses. I couldn't escape. They always greeted me in the morning with a cup of coffee and *no* conversation.

I occasionally called from the offsite, the special building in Lansing where Phil and I had first met Mark Fisk. From this building, Dianne Byrum and Mark Fisk had masterminded the Democratic takeover of the House in 2006. Now it functioned as a site from which to do various statewide political work. It was a good place for me to call—and call, and call.

This was the drill: "This is Mary Valentine. I'm running for state representative. Can I count on you for a contribution?"

Dial again, ask again. For hours on end.

My advisors pushed me harder. "It's not enough just to ask, Mary," they'd insist. "You have to pin down the person to an amount. And you have to find out exactly when they are sending it."

David Farhat's supporters, backed by state Republicans, had by then started tearing me down, throwing all kinds of misinformation out to the voters. We incorporated their malarkey into our own fundraising letters so that voters would see for themselves what kind of a campaign they were running.

All of this took a good deal of time—and expense. We'd send out hundreds of letters at a time, which meant hours of folding, stuffing, sealing, and stamping. Sometimes my family helped with these mailings, and sometimes dedicated volunteers took it upon themselves. Even my 90-year-old mom relished the opportunity to help with this job. A few days after the letters went out, I would restart the calling cycle. The ideal scenario was for folks to send the money in without needing to be called—many people did that, and I always deeply appreciated it.

I learned the basic rule of fundraising: no calls, no money, no campaign. I don't know of anybody, including me, who actually likes this process. But without funds, without donations, only the wealthy have a say in how our government is run.[10]

During the first campaign for state representative, I raised a total of around $170,000. The second campaign was closer to $200,000. While running for state senator, I raised roughly $230,000. So within a space of six years, and without any prior experience at fundraising, I brought in approximately $600,000—largely by calling and asking.

One thing that motivated me to keep going was how nasty my opponents became. I've already discussed the David Farhat campaign, which had launched a particularly vicious attack against his previous opponent, with all sorts of wild accusations. We used those attacks to generate energy for our own campaign. We blew up photos and articles, put them on poster boards, and took them to all of our fundraisers and house parties. People were appalled by the nastiness and I really think this inspired them to dig a little deeper when it came time to give.

This method became even more effective when the accusations were about me. One radio ad proclaimed: *Mary Valentine has ties to Iraqi terrorists.* The other side circulated literature that called me cruel and dangerous because I supported a plan to better fund our schools. One piece called me a liar; I'm not sure what they were basing it on, but there it was. So we used it in our own campaign to encourage donations.

We also quoted heavily from the Farhat campaign in the fundraising letters we sent out. We used the lemons our opponents threw into our path to make lemonade.

The second state representative race was more complicat-

---

[10] Sadly, that has only gotten worse. In December 2013 the Republican legislature voted to double the amount of money individual candidates and PACs are allowed to raise.

ed, because my opponent, Holly Hughes, was—and still is—a multimillionaire and could outspend us at every turn. Even more challenging, she was a National Committeewoman for the Republican Party, which meant she could get "earned media" in droves (earned media is media that comes across as news rather than political advertising, which makes it free to the campaign). We used her status as a multimillionaire Republican to raise more money, hoping my status as the financial underdog would work in our favor.

At the end of the summer during the first election, a supporter of my campaign commented that I seemed to have raised $18,000 out of thin air. It hardly seemed this way to me; I had spent several hours a day, every day of the week, asking for money. My supporters couldn't get rid of me. I even heard that I now had a reputation in Lansing for being a "pit bull" when it came to asking for money. I didn't mind hearing this. My reward for such persistence was the priceless opportunity of serving two terms in the state legislature.

Independent Political Action Committees (PACs) at that time could give $5,000 for the House campaign and up to $10,000 for the Senate campaign. Individual donors could give $500 for the House race and $1,000 for the Senate race. (Those numbers have now doubled, as noted earlier.) The idea was to get people to "max out" during the election cycle. Many did this $25, $50, or $100 at a time. I noticed in all three races that my Republican opponents had an easier job convincing donors to "max out" than I did. They had a significantly higher number of donors who wrote out checks for $500 or $1,000 right off the bat, so the candidate could then contact other potential donors. They simply had a higher number of wealthy donors. Since Democrats include a high number of middle- and working-class people who get out of bed every morning and head off to a not-so-high-paying job, they give in smaller allotments, out of necessity. Even the PACs that "maxed out" to me couldn't do it all at once. The environmental organizations that supported me raised their money gradually from citizens who cared about environmental issues.

Unions that supported me also raised their money one small donation at a time from hard-working people. Same with Planned Parenthood, EMILY's List, MiList, and the Progressive Women's Alliance, all of which supported me. The big money PACs are the Chamber of Commerce, Michigan Manufacturing, and the Farm Bureau, none of which support Democrats, as a rule. Add to that the fact that I actually voted for what I believed in and stood up to the big guys on behalf of my constituents, and it's a bit of a miracle that I won a second term as state representative.

All of this explains why state Republicans came after me so viciously when I ran for Senate. They simply couldn't afford to let a woman like me—someone who had already stood up for what she believed in when it came to education reform, women's rights, working families, and environmental responsibility, get into the Senate. What would the world come to?

Taking much-needed money from PACs was crucial for my successes, though I had mixed feelings about it. I knew I needed more money than I could get from individuals in order to win, but I didn't want anyone to think they owned me. Sometimes it felt like a worrisome dilemma. When you get right down to it, though, people shouldn't make political donations to "own" a legislator. They should be giving because they have a philosophy and values in common with the potential legislator. Ideally, voters would expect the public figure to research, talk to constituents, and then make sound decisions—ones that would be good for the citizens back home. My donors were wonderful and always honored that. Blessedly, no donors ever came back to me and said I owed them a vote because they had donated to my campaign.

Anonymous contributors to the MLive comment section pushed the idea that I was bought and paid for by the teachers' unions. That notion is simply not true. I've worked in enough schools to know that teachers are hardworking and deserve good pay, that "merit pay" is a ridiculous notion that won't benefit students, and that tenure, though not perfect, is a good thing because it gives teachers confidence to do the right thing and lends stability to schools. I ran to support those ideas and would have supported them even if the teachers' unions hadn't given me a dime.

I disagreed with the unions on one issue—that of mental health parity, or equal coverage for mental health services. I've always been a strong supporter of treating mental health needs equally with other health needs. In my own life, I have benefitted greatly from access to medication for depression. And I believe that providing treatment for mental health issues and addiction costs citizens less in the long run. When left untreated, those illnesses become far more costly for the entire society. But unions, by and large, thought those issues should be covered in local contracts rather than state law. I didn't buy it and parted with all the unions on that issue. And I voted accordingly.

Looking back on my experiences with political fundraising, I have to say that I wish having a wealthy campaign wasn't such a clear advantage for a candidate. Until we can cap how much money people can use their own money in campaigns, though, I don't see any way around it. If I'm limited, and the millionaire running against me has no limits, we won't have equal footing. The solution is for voters to pay close attention, ignore the ridiculous advertisements, and donate what they can when they find someone trustworthy and determined to make positive change.

I can also report that, as Election Day neared, a wonderful thing happened in my first campaign; the fundraising took on a life of its own. All those months of making calls brought contributions in daily and I could concentrate on the final leg of the campaign: getting our supporters to the polls.

Chapter VIII

Bottom of the Ninth

The election for the state senate seat was months ago. The anger in my gut has been replaced with a profound epiphany—that losing definitely had an upside. I started as an activist and gained experience and knowledge through the years. Had I won, though I certainly would relish being a state senator, I would have been powerless serving in the minority. As an advocate for everyday people and someone who has served in the state legislature, I now can use my contacts and knowledge in my ongoing life as an activist. And I'm so happy to take part fully in family life again.

On a personal level, it's because I was no longer serving in the legislature that I had more time to spend with my mom during her final days. I have also had a chance to get to know my two precious granddaughters while they are still babies, an opportunity I'll always treasure.

Still, everything I experienced in office was incredible—an experience I also deeply value.

I was 59 years old when I won my first election. I brought a wealth of life experiences with me: working as a speech pathologist for 30 years, parenting, traveling, earning a Bachelor and Master's Degree, becoming a published author, teaching Sunday school, raising two children, being an out-

doorswoman. Not to mention the life changes that divorce and relocation bring. Not many things surprise me anymore.

But nothing in any of my life experiences prepared me for those last two weeks before that first Election Day.

* * * *

How to explain my emotions as November 7, 2006, drew near? The best comparison I can make is a baseball analogy: You are cheering for your favorite team in the World Series. The score is tied. It is the bottom of the ninth, your team is up, and the count is full. The tension is so thick, you suspect you're going to jump out of your skin at any moment. Eventually, though, the players play, win or lose the game, and the tension ends—either in elation or disappointment.

But for me, it was like this each day and night for the last two weeks of the campaign. Normal sleep went out the window, replaced by tossing and turning, wondering what would happen next. Would all the months of excruciatingly hard work pay off? The polls looked good. Polls can be wrong, though. We heard great things from voters as we did our last minute door-to-door canvassing. Still, you never know how people will actually vote. The last thing I wanted was to get overly confident, only to have my hopes dashed with a loss. I fought my own hopefulness. The fact is that candidates from my party had been ahead in this district before, but the spate of last-minute negative ads at the end had cost them the election. The same thing could easily happen to me.

Our campaign headquarters was an empty storefront in the old Kmart Plaza on Henry Street in Norton Shores. It consisted of one long room in the front of the space lined with long tables with phones on them, ready for the hours of phone banking we did. A room at the back was furnished with a refrigerator and an old dining room table hauled out of our basement, which was always filled with food and coffee, and cluttered with dishes and empty cups. Two desks held computers for scanning information, and a glass dining room table served for campaign meetings. Walk sheets—the lists of targeted voters—were everywhere, piled on tables and desks, still in boxes, stacked on the floor.

Before we moved into our headquarters in May 2006, we had to clean it, paint it, and even rebuild the ceiling. The rear door needed continual fixing, and the back room was a tad musty. We had many memorable times in that old building, not the least of which was our grand opening event, where we celebrated the official beginning of the campaign. So much camaraderie and excitement filled that space. And occasional conflict, too—like the time I argued with my staff about whether or not to advertise my hard-won endorsement from the Michigan Education Association (MEA) with a press release.

Because of my limited background in politics, I thought it would be a foregone conclusion that I would receive an endorsement from the MEA. After all, I was a lifetime member and my opponent was certainly no friend of education. But David Farhat, an extremely clever politician, from what I understand, almost outfoxed me to get that endorsement. He pretty much voted against education at every opportunity throughout his terms in office, but after he realized a teacher was running against him, he changed his tune. I was told that he made a deal with an MEA lobbyist to vote to protect MESSA insurance if the lobbyist would see to it that David received the MEA endorsement. Endorsements are decided by the local Screening and Recommendation (S & R) group, so the lobbyist really had no business making such a promise. But the lobbyist promised anyway, and did everything in his power to get the S & R team to endorse my opponent. After we learned what had been promised to Farhat, we worked diligently to earn the endorsement, but there were no guarantees. There was some fear that if MEA did *not* endorse Farhat—and if he won the election—he would retaliate and vote against MEA issues at every turn.

But guess what? The MEA members went against their lobbyist and gave me the endorsement. When I announced this to the team assembled at the headquarters, we broke into cheers and had an impromptu champagne toast. We were all relieved and encouraged by this development. The Republican Party would have had a field day if David Farhat had won the endorsement of my own organization. In the end, we decided against making a public announcement. Although I believe that a strong union leads to a strong education system for the students, not everyone agrees with me, and my staff felt it could hurt me politically.

I was at the headquarters when my staff and I learned the results of a baseline poll that had been given in August 2006, after months of campaigning. Poll results are a tense moment in any campaign, akin to receiving a score on a vital exam or an evaluation that determines your pay. This poll was no different. As a candidate I had poured my heart and soul into getting to know the voters and sharing my vision with them. Polls give the results of all that work, and the outcome often rests on these results. No one wants to donate money to a losing campaign, so supporters often look at the polls to determine where they will spend their money.

In creating the polls, the campaign consultants need to determine what negatives about either candidate are likely to come out during the campaign. So they start by asking some generic questions about each candidate.

"Have you ever heard of Mary Valentine?"

"Do you have negative feelings about her?"

"Do you have positive feelings about her?"

"Have you ever heard of David Farhat?"

And so on.

Then the pollsters ask a whole litany of questions designed to reveal flaws about both candidates. Then come more questions about the candidates. The goal is to come out of the poll in the lead, even after the poll has listed some unflattering flaws.

Coincidentally, the pollsters called a couple of people from my campaign, including my brother Doug.

"I know those things aren't true about Mary Valentine," he said when the caller came to the part of the poll containing unflattering items. He was so upset that he couldn't finish the poll and hung up on the caller. His loyalty still makes me smile when I think about it.

The two weeks of waiting to receive the results of that first poll were excruciating. Finally, the call came. Several of us huddled in the back room on a conference call with Mark Fisk. He had incredible news. We were ahead in the polls by 18 points: a significant lead. I was so thrilled and elated that my feet wouldn't touch the ground. Everyone else on the call had worked just as hard as I had and they were floating to the ceiling with me.

At that time, we didn't want the word to get out that we were that far ahead. We needed to keep the momentum high and continue to run like we were ten points behind. I understood this, but it was really hard for me to keep quiet about it. Later that same day I knocked on doors in a Norton Shores neighborhood, wanting to shout at everyone I met: "We're ahead in the polls! We're ahead in the polls!" Instead, I introduced myself and listened as calmly as possible.

Inside, though, I felt different. It was hard to wipe the grin off my face even when talking to voters about something serious.

Tracking polls continued throughout the fall to keep on top of how the campaign was going. During the final weeks of the campaign, our ancient, decrepit headquarters on Henry Street also was the site of a midnight rescue mission. At that point in the campaign, the deputy campaign manager was Jeff Rector, who first came on board when we were still working out of my house in Norton Shores. Jeff was a recent graduate of the James Madison School of Michigan State University, bright and extremely hard working. The previous June he had set up his computer at our kitchen table and had begun working for me without hesitation. In fact, he was like an honorary member of my family.

In August, Eric Samuelson, our EMILY'S List campaign worker, had also joined the team. Eric is probably the most single-minded person I have ever known. Eric had received the job of recruiting volunteers. For two solid hours every morning, he called potential volunteers. "Mary Valentine, someone you can trust," was how he ended every message he left. I can still hear his voice saying those words.

Late one October night, Jeff and Eric were still at headquarters along with our organizer, Mike, when a ferocious storm blew in off Lake Michigan. A gust of wind caught the unlocked front door and whipped it open with a vengeance. It smashed against the huge plate-glass window at the front of the headquarters, breaking it into a million pieces.

Their call woke me from a sound sleep. My husband, Phil, along with Chris and the three young men, went to work immediately, building a temporary replacement right then, in the middle of the night. My husband found some old plywood boards he had been saving for just such an emergency and dragged them down to the office. Chris took charge and the team boarded up the window. It was one of those moments I was glad to have Chris Kilgroe at the helm, with his background as an engineer.

It was a good thing campaign workers were at the office when the window shattered. Everyone who came into the headquarters suspected it was the work of Republicans; even some Republicans wondered about that. I might have been tempted to think that as well, if I hadn't known what really happened.

The Sunday before the first Election Day was particularly tough. David Farhat placed a full-page ad in the *Muskegon Chronicle* outlining all the things his family had done for the Muskegon community and claiming that my campaign had smeared his name and that of his good-hearted family. Chris and I were putting up a large Mary Valentine sign on McCracken Avenue in Norton Shores when someone called us to tell us about the ad. Terrified, we immediately called Mark Fisk for guidance.

"Newspaper is the most ineffective form of political advertising," he told us calmly. "Don't worry about it."

I tried not to worry, but I was already aware of a surge in ugly campaign literature. Farhat's ad in the *Chronicle* was one more to add to the pile. I wasn't so sure of how voters would respond to his accusations. It brought my own anxiety about the election to an almost unbearable level.

The Monday night before the election was a highlight of the entire campaign. On November 5th, a massive rally was held for Governor Jennifer Granholm (who was seeking reelection) at Fricano's, a popular pizza joint on Western Avenue in Muskegon. Fricano's consists of one large dining room and on that night, people were packed to the walls, tight as sardines. The crowd was jubilant and couldn't wait to see the governor. I saw many familiar faces—both old and new friends. Everyone running for office was pushed to the front of the room to speak to our supporters while we waited for Governor Granholm. A small group of Girl Scouts wormed their way to the front of the room where I was standing and asked for my signature. It was a heady moment.

When it was my turn to speak, the room went wild.

Before my run for office, I would have been hiding at the back of the room rather than taking my place on center stage. The experience of connecting so joyfully with a crowd of people was completely new to me—and wonderful. It helped prepare me for everything that would happen the next day.

Then it was November 6th, 2006: Election Day.

The heart and soul of our campaign had been making sure our supporters got to the polls to vote. Stage one of our Get-Out-The-Vote effort was chasing our supporters who were voting absentee, a successful venture headed up by my daughter, Robin. Stage two was Election Day. During the weeks leading up to the campaign, volunteer recruitment for Election Day had intensified. On Election Day, we had hundreds of people on hand to help get voters to the polls. The mechanism we had created to ensure a good turnout was running well.

It was harder for me personally. I had a hard time figuring out what to do with myself as the day wore on. I decided to go with my son, Shawn, to a voting site in Fruitport and spend some time shaking the hands of voters, handing them a final piece of campaign literature, and answering any questions they might have. This was completely legal as long as we were 100 feet away from the front door of the polling place. Shawn and I made sure we were 200 feet from the front door, just to be on the safe side.

"How can a Sunday School teacher be for abortion?" one man asked.

"I'm not *for* abortion," I answered for the zillionth time. "Instead of fighting about it, though, I think we should find common ground and develop effective solutions. One thing we know for sure is that criminalizing abortions doesn't eliminate them—and doesn't even decrease them. Why would we want such an ineffective strategy?"

The man was friendly after our discussion. I was glad to clarify my position one last time and I had the distinct feeling I had won his vote.

Suddenly a man pulled up to the front of the polling place, jumped out of his car, and started yelling.

"You're too close to that door!" he hollered. He repeated this several times and glared at us angrily when he passed us to enter the building. Soon we noticed that voters were chuckling about this same man as they came back outside. Seems he caused quite a commotion inside the polling place, yelling about how someone needed to go outside with a tape measure because I was standing too close to the door. He yelled to everyone within earshot that Mary Valentine was breaking the law.

Officials at the site came outside and measured the distance. Of course we were legal—by a long shot. As this was happening, the same man sat in his car and glared at us. Soon David Farhat himself rolled by in a giant, gas-guzzling vehicle. Next, a police officer showed up and warned us not to go any closer to the door, as though we were behaving like criminals. Another person with a camera began taking pictures of us as though collecting "evidence."

We stood our ground, but when these assorted bullies eventually left, Shawn and I were so shook up that we needed to return to headquarters to calm down.

Later, it was reported to me that the Farhat team spent Election Day driving around town pulling our signs out of the ground and putting his signs in their place.

Late in the afternoon, I rested, in hopes this would make time pass more quickly. It didn't work. The final hours dragged. At 8:00 p.m., after the polls closed, volunteers and campaign staff gathered at the headquarters. Volunteers worked in each polling place calling in precinct vote totals as they were counted and registered. The headquarter walls were covered with reporting forms. Someone posted every reported vote total on the wall, and every single time, we had earned more votes than we had targeted to achieve the win. A number came in, a cheer went up. We got louder and crazier as the evening wore on. I cannot remember a louder, more in-your-face, thrilling moment in my life. My marriage to Phil Valentine and the birth of my children, of course, were the most thrilling. But they were quieter. This was a yell, scream, and   jump-up-and-down-and-hug-the-guy-next-to-you thrilling experience.

And I simply couldn't stop laughing.

Eventually, we left the headquarters and found our way to the Democratic Victory Party at Pulaski Hall, where the celebration continued. My mom and siblings and cousins were there, along with friends, good Democrats, campaign supporters, and folks from other campaigns. I think I hugged every person in the hall that night.

My victory was in fact a landslide: 56% - 44%. We accomplished the impossible; an unknown newcomer defeated a two-term incumbent named Farhat in Muskegon County.

At one point I remember that my throat was parched from yelling, but when I tried to walk to the bar to get a glass of pop, it took me about half an hour because so many wonderful well-wishers and celebrators stopped me along the way. And there was more thrilling news later in the evening, when we learned that Democrats would be in the majority in the House of Representatives. I will never forget the sight of Mike Blake running across the room, shouting with joy when he realized the magnitude of our victory.

After months of fighting to get media attention, suddenly there it was. The news media were there in full force, and I did several interviews that night. Photographers were snapping and cameras were rolling. It was a moment I never expected to experience in my lifetime.

One photograph from election night captures it all. It is a picture of my sister Maggie, my mom, and I standing side by side, with Maggie's fist held high in victory. We all wore wide grins, but mine was over the top. I looked slightly crazed. On that amazing night, sharing my victory with family, friends, and loyal staff, it was simply impossible for me to contain my joy.

My mom, Phyllis Hostetler, me in the middle and my sister Maggie
Hostetler, celebrating our victory, Nov. '06.

Chapter IX

Caucus

It's the first winter of my return to "civilian life," as my friend Dave Gitchell calls it, and today there is too much snow for me to make the drive to my spot at the café. In fact, I haven't seen this much snow since I left Michigan's Upper Peninsula in 1980. It's been snowing for weeks. Will we ever have a melting day?

I woke up thinking about the Senate campaign—wondering what we could have done differently, reviewing both my mistakes and my opponent's mean-spirited campaign. It's not as hard for me to do that now, but some mornings I still feel a knot of anger in my gut. Like this morning.

I am thinking about the woman who followed me as state representative in the 91st District: multi-millionaire Holly Hughes. Every time she blinks, it appears, her name pops up in the newspaper. She receives constant coverage. Sometimes I think they must have some kind of contest to see which reporter can mention her most often. When I think of the tremendous amount of work I had to do to get even a bit of "earned media," I can't help it—I feel angry and frustrated. I worked so hard. I started from scratch. I pushed and pushed to open the door a wee bit. Holly Hughes taps on the door once and it flies open. I know these feelings will pass, but today I resent the woman who replaced me.

Then I have a brighter memory, one that erases the anger

*and puts a smile on my face. It's 2006 again. I am thinking of
my colleagues in the caucus, whom I came to love.*

*Initially, though, it was quite an adjustment. Even before
my team had put the yard signs into storage, even before I
learned to answer to the title of state representative, an ordeal
unfolded in Lansing that was unlike anything I had experienced in my professional life. I had been elected and it was
time for our party to choose our caucus leaders.*

* * * *

The drama started immediately. As representative-elect
from the 91st District, I was joining the state House after an
election that had created a Democratic majority. Our newly
elected leader would become the new speaker of the house.
Our floor leader would become the majority floor leader. Once
chosen, they would become two of the most powerful government officials in the state, so electing them was a grueling
process—especially for someone like me, unused to the inner
workings of state politics.

The political pressure started early. Everyone running for
any leadership position had come to my district and knocked
on doors on my behalf. They had made significant donations
to my tough and expensive political campaign. They had
become my friends. I didn't want to seem ungrateful to any of
them. Whom would I chose? Would I make permanent
enemies of those I didn't vote for? Would I be undone by in-
house politics and expectations before I even got started?
These questions were going through my mind as I drove to
Lansing two days after the election for that first caucus
meeting—and the election of our leaders.

The contest quickly narrowed to two teams: Team Dil-
lon/Tobocman, and Team Meisner/Wheeler-Smith. Steve

Tobocman was seen as a progressive leader and Andy Dillon as a conservative. The other team was far more clearly in the progressive corner—Andy Meisner, state representative from Ferndale, was running for speaker, and Alma Wheeler-Smith, former state senator from the Ann Arbor area, for the position of majority floor leader.

Many stood in caucus and gave speeches for their favorite candidate. The procedure was new to me after all my years of working with children, and I was initially taken aback by the formality of the speeches.

"I rise today to nominate Andy Dillon to be our leader," began Representative Paul Condino. Before that moment, I had never heard anyone say they rose to do anything. In pre-school, actually, you rarely rose at all. Generally, you sat on the floor and talked in short sentences, which was a bit different from what I was experiencing now.

Andy Dillon announced that he had a secret plan for the budget. Andy Meisner's speech was about core progressive values. In the end, Dillon squeaked out a win and ran the show for two terms. Steve Tobocman, who became majority floor leader for his final term before he was term-limited out of office, played a big part in determining which pieces of legislation would come up for a vote. The speaker pro tem ran the daily sessions.

During my first term, that job went to Mike Sak of Grand Rapids, who ran the chamber with a rare passion. I remember vividly the last day of the 2007-08 session in mid-December. The voting started at 10:00 a.m. on a Thursday morning. Speaker Pro Tem Sak stuck with the job all night long, bringing up bill after bill for a vote. He still looked rarin' to go when the session finally ended 25 hours later—at 11:00 a.m. Friday morning. During my second term, Pam Byrnes, from Washtenaw County's 52nd District, served as speaker pro tem. She, too, did an amazing job and was generous about sharing that position with younger representatives.

Andy Dillon is one of the most charming people I know, in a reserved and handsome sort of way—and an astute politician. I always enjoyed working with him when he was the speaker. But in my opinion, his Republican leanings never left him, and even intensified during his second year as speaker. After that, he even served in a Republican administration.

During my first term, however, the team of Dillon and Steve Tobocman worked well—truly a balance of conservatism and progressive values. As a result, the party was able to pass significant clean water and energy legislation. The Chamber of Commerce and the Farm Bureau, which control many legislators, didn't like the legislation, so the bills contained many weaknesses—but it was a start.

The word "caucus" is part of the political vernacular in every state of the union. Although politicians use the word often, the average citizen doesn't necessarily understand it. The *American Heritage College Dictionary* defines the word "caucus" as: *a meeting of the local members of a political party, especially to select delegates to a convention.* Or this: *a closed meeting of party members within a legislative body.* Or finally: *a group within a legislative body seeking to represent a specific interest or influence a policy area.*

A ubiquitous word, "caucus" means different things at different times, depending on the context. For instance, when I say something happened "in caucus," I am referring to the closed meeting of party members within a legislative body. Yet when I talk about "the caucus," it's the party I'm referring to. Despite this seeming confusion, everybody in the political world understands what is meant—one of many political paradoxes.

At the Capitol Building, our caucus meetings were held in a special room off the main chamber (where the entire House gathers) when we were in session. To get to the Democratic caucus room, I would walk past the wide podium at the front of the chamber where the speaker pro tem stood with his gavel (running the session) and continue on past the clerks (the main clerk and a wide variety of lesser clerks, all busily registering and archiving bills and amendments). I then would exit a door at the back of the chamber, turn left down a narrow hallway, and enter the caucus room. The Republican caucus room is, as you might guess, down a hallway to the right.

The caucus room is long and narrow, with a massive table in the middle that nearly fills it. Some chairs are pulled up to the table and others line the perimeter of the room. A large, ornate chandelier hangs overhead, with tall windows along three sides. The room is in the same late nineteenth-century décor as the rest of the capital, which was restored to its original charm in the late 1990s. The caucus chair sits at the head of the table with a gavel. Leadership also sits toward the front of the room. The other caucus members choose seats wherever they're comfortable. I tended to sit near Representative Marie Donigan, from Royal Oak, and Representative Bob Jones, from Kalamazoo.

The leader calls caucuses whenever he or she needs to consult with the other members. The caucus chair comes to the podium microphone in the chamber during a session on the House floor to announce the meeting.

As in: "Democrats, time for caucus."

Or "Republicans, please come to the caucus room."

My first term, Representative Mo Hood from Detroit was the person who called the Democrats to caucus, and during my second term, it was Representative Barb Byrum.

I quickly learned about an interesting juxtaposition. As state representatives, we were warned never to repeat what we had discussed in caucus. Yet the news media sat nearby, just inside the main chamber, hoping that someone would spill the beans as soon as we finished our meeting and they would get a choice morsel of news. Whenever one of us walked into or out of the caucus room, we stopped talking, to prevent anyone just outside the door from eavesdropping. Secrecy was important to keep fragile negotiations between the House and Senate chambers from falling apart. Secrecy also allowed us to discuss more freely the various aspects of bills and issues without fearing it would be used against us in the next campaign. But as I quickly learned, the details of our meetings often found their way to the media anyway. It was puzzling.

The caucus meetings were sometimes dry and boring. At other times, they were emotional and dramatic—sometimes excruciatingly so. We spilled our guts, disagreed, broke into tears, and yelled at one another over particularly heartfelt issues.

Mayor Dave Bing came to our caucus to reveal his plans for the future of Detroit shortly after he was elected. Governor Jennifer Granholm met with us from time to time—often to share her ideas for resolving the endless state budget crisis.

Perhaps the most divisive and emotional issue we faced as a caucus was the abortion debate. The most dramatic discussion came when Michigan Right-To-Life (RTL) descended on the capitol to present a bill intended to criminalize something that is already illegal: Intact Dilation and Extraction, which, according to the AMA House of Delegates, is the medical term for what RTL calls partial birth abortion. (*Wikipedia* describes it as a form of abortion in which the cervix is dilated and the fetus extracted in pieces using surgical forceps in the case of a late-term miscarriage or abortion.) The AMA recommends that the procedure be used only when alternative procedures pose greater risk to the woman, and only within standards of good medical practice and in the best interest of the patient. In the year 2000, when it was still legal, it was used in 0.17% of all abortions, according to the Alan Guttmacher Institute.

This issue came back to Lansing each year strictly for political reasons. Everyone knew that Governor Granholm, concerned about the health of women, would veto it. Both at the national and state level, the RTL organization uses this inflated controversy as an opportunity to show their donors they're doing something big in the realm of politics. Legislators who go along with this pretense can win easy points with their conservative base.

Let me back up for a moment. The Michigan RTL organization has a serious claim on the legislators they endorse. Legislators in Lansing who have received an endorsement from them go straight to the RTL lobbyist, Ed Rivet, for instructions on how to vote on any issue related to abortion— including sex education, birth control, and adoption. These public servants don't think through the bills or ask questions of their constituents to gain a deeper understanding of the complexity of the issue. They turn to their lobbyist and do what they are told.

Intact D & X was developed to save the life and health of the mother in rare and heartbreaking situations. The procedure is used only when no safe alternative exists. A bill to ban the procedure (though it is already illegal across the country because of a Supreme Court ruling and is no longer legally performed) came before the caucus in my first term. The "talking point" RTL used with their constituents was that criminalizing this procedure at the state level was necessary in case the Supreme Court ruling was ever overturned. Every medical organization in the entire state opposed the bill as it was written. But emotions ran high. When we discussed its pros and cons, fellow legislators put their deepest-held feelings on the caucus table. It was an agonizing session that left us disturbed and divided.

Republican leadership needed the bill to come up for a vote to gain more votes for their members in the next election. According to Speaker Andy Dillon, the Republican minority promised essentially to use the power of their minority to shut the legislature down and render it totally useless unless the bill was brought up for a vote while their supporters were in Lansing.

In the end, Speaker Dillon did bring it up for a vote. It passed and was subsequently vetoed by Governor Granholm. I voted against it. I studied it in depth, looking at the pros and at the cons. In the end, I decided I simply didn't have the medical expertise to make this decision for every woman in the state of Michigan in every situation. For the life of me, I cannot figure out how untrained legislators think they should overrule doctors and families who are making such difficult health decisions.

Few in the House opposed this bill. When the votes went up on the board and increasingly more green votes popped up, I felt anger in my gut. It seemed clear to me that those who supported this legislation didn't care about my health, my daughter's health, or the health of Michigan women. I simply couldn't support the bill. I discovered later that this vote made me a villain to some—but a bit of a hero to the policy people in the back room. They admired my courage in making that tough, unpopular vote so early in my term. I

Billboards from '10 Senate Election

suspect that was when the political analyst Brenda Lawson formed the opinion that I was a true stateswoman.

Years later, that controversial vote was used against me in my Senate campaign. An offshoot of the Education Action Group (EAG) put up a series of huge, well-placed, bright-red billboards in the parts of the Senate district where I was least known. The billboards proclaimed: Mary Valentine Supports Partial Birth Abortion.

One woman who saw that billboard called me to express her views.

"I don't *support* partial birth abortion," I told her.

"Well, you'd better take that billboard down, then," she suggested. "Because it's misleading." I bit my tongue. Apparently, the woman thought I had put the billboard up and could easily take it down. And when I mentioned that birth control was the best deterrent to abortion, she made it clear that she didn't believe in birth control either. In her view, if women could use birth control, they would become promiscuous and unfaithful to their husbands.

I can't even begin to comment on this except to say that this is what we are up against and why voter education is critical.

During the budget crisis of 2007, we legislators practically lived in the Capitol Building. I spent many hours with my fellow representatives in the caucus room discussing solutions and strategies: *Should we make massive cuts? Should we raise some taxes? Or perhaps a combination of the two? What about the political repercussions? Can we, as elected officials, do the right thing by raising revenues a bit (taxes) and continue working on the issues that brought us here? Or will we be thrown out of office by recall elections (which I will describe in greater depth later in this book)?*

These weren't easy questions, but we struggled to find solutions and common ground in that caucus room. But sometimes, being in caucus was actually enjoyable. During one meeting, our colleague from the Upper Peninsula, Representative Steve Lindbergh, revealed his true identity to us— right in the midst of a heartfelt discussion about school funding. Our expressions had turned serious, and the tone of our voices had become strained. Steve stood to make a point. Then, to our surprise, he started undressing! First, he unbuckled his belt, pulled it free and threw it on the floor. Then he unbuttoned his top shirt button, and the next one, and the one after that, until his shirt was completely unbuttoned. We were stunned into silence. He then removed his shirt and threw it down. Instead of his bare chest, we saw a bright red t-shirt with a blue Y in the middle along with the word, "*YOOPERMAN!*" Steve gave us the comic relief we needed at that moment.

In 2007, our caucus was closely knit. Newly in the majority, we pulled together across differences in ideology and geography to make good decisions for Michigan. With the Republican Senate fighting us every step of the way, it was tough, but we moved legislation to keep Michigan's water in Michigan. We worked to create a renewable portfolio standard—weak, but a standard nonetheless, intended to clean up the air and bring jobs to Michigan. We were able to bring revenues in to keep critical public services alive.

We also passed good legislation that subsequently got stuck in the Senate: a no-reason absentee ballot bill, bills that would stop out-of-state trash from pouring into our state, and legislation to reverse the complete immunity from prosecution that big drug companies receive in the state of Michigan.

I didn't always agree with Andy Dillon, but I must give him credit for getting at least some of these good pieces of legislation passed into law. The others? No-reason absentee voting and ending out-of-state trash and drug immunity? I suspect the voters will have to flip the Senate to Democrats if they ever want those common-sense bills passed into law.

As we worked on these and other bills, we developed a bond that can only come from working so hard together—one that I believe will continue forever.

My second term in office was quite different. Our caucus was much larger and Speaker Dillon also was running for governor, which made him more distant and caused some resentment, particularly among our new members. For example, the speaker used his political wisdom to trick caucus members into participating in the demise of the Michigan Promise.

The Michigan Promise was a scholarship built upon the Michigan Merit Award, which had been adopted in Michigan initially in 1999. In 2006, under the Granholm administration, it was re-named the Michigan Promise and expanded, so more money could go to students who completed their first two years of college and went on to work on a Bachelor's Degree. To earn this scholarship, students had to do well on their junior year standardized testing. The purpose of the reconstituted Michigan Promise was twofold: first, to encourage students to work hard in school so they would do well on their testing; second, to grow the number of college graduates in Michigan.

A clear correlation exists between the number of college graduates in a state and the employment number. Consistently, states with more college graduates have a lower rate of unemployment. For more than 100 years, Michigan's economy was based on manufacturing, so for many generations Michigan's young people had been able to get good-paying jobs right out of high school. As a result, a culture that assumed college was unnecessary has grown in our state. Clearly, though, that culture must change to bring Michigan successfully into the 21st century. The Michigan Promise was a step toward doing that.

But with the demise of Michigan's manufacturing also came the demise of our once-healthy tax base. This led to a sharp difference between Democrats and Republicans. During our flush years, the legislature had been able to cut income taxes to one of the lowest rates in the country: 3.9%. We increased that slightly during my first term, but when the worldwide economic crash hit, Michigan again had to decide how to handle the resulting drop in revenue. A small, temporary income tax increase would have resolved the issue, allowing us to fully fund our schools and continue turning around Michigan's anti-education culture.

While I was serving in Lansing, the Republican Party operated under the firm belief that any tax increase for any reason is always wrong—whether intended to benefit roads, education, or even public health. This made it all the more surprising that when they took office in 2010, they raised taxes. But since they raised taxes only on the poor, the old, and middle-class families, they could protect their wealthy donors. Strangely, though, they didn't use the extra money to provide services to citizens. Regardless, when I was serving in Lansing and the Republicans were working to get into the majority, they didn't dare increase taxes for any reason.

Which leads us back to the Michigan Promise. I, along with most other Democrats, thought we should find a way to keep it intact. The Republicans thought it should be eliminated. For a few weeks, discussion in Lansing centered on what to do with the Michigan Promise. Two branches of government, the House and the governor, were in the hands of Democrats. But with the Senate in the hands of the Republicans, the issue could potentially be stonewalled forever, stopping government cold.

We discussed many possible solutions for how to handle the Michigan Promise. Should we partially cut it? Decrease its cost by making it need based? The Senate took the matter into its own hands and presented a budget bill that completely eliminated it. For this budget to become operational, though, the Democratic House would have to pass it.

So Speaker Dillon and Senate Republican Leader Mike Bishop concocted an arrangement. If Speaker Dillon could convince his caucus to pass the budget bill with the Michigan Promise eliminated, Leader Bishop would restore the missing Michigan Promise clause when the bill came back to the Senate.

Certainly, though, nobody in Lansing thought Speaker Dillon could get his good-hearted caucus to defeat something as important to Michigan's working families as the Michigan Promise. But several of our members voted for the Senate budget that completely eliminated the Michigan Promise. Of course, the bill with no funding for the Michigan Promise passed in the Senate—and that was the end of it.

The result was that low-income students who had counted on that scholarship money were left empty-handed. And we, as elected officials, helped further shrink the middle class.

To this day, the Michigan Promise hasn't been restored. As far as I know, no one is even talking about reconstituting it. Our wealthiest citizens won't be remotely affected by the Michigan Promise's demise, which will harm only those who must struggle to make ends meet.

Why, oh why, I continuously ask myself, do Michigan voters continue to elect officials who have so little regard for their welfare?

Because of term limits (a maximum of three two-year terms for the House) and because of the upcoming state senate election, many of my colleagues were running for office during my second term—some actually running against each other in primaries. This made achieving the same sense of solidarity we had enjoyed in my first term difficult. This is another disadvantage to Michigan's ridiculously short term limits—too much focus on politics and not enough on policy.

Caucus also was the place bill sponsors explained their complex legislation to other caucus members and answered their questions. If we disagreed about how we would handle issues, one person made the final decision: the caucus leader. In our case, that was Speaker Andy Dillon. We could talk, argue, complain and explain, but in the end, decisions were left with Speaker Dillon, hopefully tempered by the rest of the leadership team, which included the majority floor leader and the speaker pro tem. The speaker also determines what bills will be brought up in committee or come up for a vote on the chamber floor. Andy was good about giving committee chairs a great deal of leeway to run their own committees—but in the end, if he wanted something stopped, it stopped. The power of the caucus leader is tremendous, and the power of the speaker, even more so.

Although I didn't always agree with Speaker Dillon—and still don't—I don't believe he ever engaged in the abuse of power we've seen from Jase Bolger, Republican representing the 63rd district and the speaker following Andy Dillon's tenure. Speaker Bolger and his caucus got caught attempting to silence members who were simply trying to represent their districts. Further, he became entangled in election fraud that got him into hot water with Kent County's prosecutor and even resulted in a grand jury investigation.

A caucus also can be a group to inform or persuade for a particular issue. One caucus I joined early in my first term was the "talent caucus," led by Senator Gilda Jacobs and Representative Andy Meisner, which taught legislators about the value of talent in bringing jobs to our state. Studies indicate that in today's job market, the jobs follow the talent. That's why Google (along with its cadre of jobs) located in Ann Arbor, Michigan, in September 2006. The multi-cultural, progressive city of Ann Arbor attracts talented young people, and Google took advantage of this resource. Google didn't come to Michigan because of our tax structure; they came for the talented young workers they knew they would find once they had a base in the Ann Arbor area. The Google executives were clear about that—which demonstrates how important a well-educated population is to job growth.

There were other caucuses as well—caucuses of all stripes. Generally, a caucus met at noontime when legislators were available for a gathering. Most often we met in the Mackinac Room, on the fifth floor of the House Office Building, which was also the bridge between the north and south buildings. The Mackinac Room has a striking mural of the Mackinac Bridge on one wall. Lunch was always offered at the back of the room. After we had selected our food, we would listen to a presentation.

I took all the information that came my way to heart, and voted according to what I learned. This, I quickly realized, wasn't what most of my colleagues did. From what I could tell, many legislators—particularly those on the other side of the aisle—voted based on preconceived notions rather than anything they learned from the experts, whether or not those notions were based in fact. Legislators are often too invested in ideology, or those funding their campaign, or however their leaders had instructed them to vote. I'm sorry to report that time and again, what those legislators learned from various educational caucuses was largely irrelevant to how they voted.

A caucus is also the term for a meeting at which local parties elect their leaders. In Muskegon County, for example, our Democratic meetings were held at the CIO Hall on Western Avenue in downtown Muskegon while I was serving in the legislature.

In the political world, everything is a caucus. For instance, the Bipartisan Smoker's Caucus met on the balcony of the Capitol Building. The Street Corner Caucus (a group of legislators discussing where to have lunch) met on the corner of Ottawa and Capitol. Last, but not least, was the Stiletto Caucus (for women legislators whose ankles have the strength to allow them to walk in those lovely, but god-awfully uncomfortable, shoes). My favorite caucus, though, was one invented by my friend Kate Ebli after we both lost our last elections: the Kicked-Out Caucus—with far too many members, in my opinion.

But for now, permit me to dwell on another incredibly happy memory—the day I was sworn into office: January 10, 2007.

Chapter X

It's Official

It's noon on January 12, 2011—the second Wednesday in January. I'm in the gallery of the House of Representatives to help celebrate Marcia Hovey-Wright's official swearing-in ceremony, the day she officially becomes state representative for Michigan's 92nd district. Constitutionally, the ceremonial swearing-in is always on the second Wednesday of the January following the election, which has been Michigan's tradition since we became the 26th state to enter the Union on January 26, 1837. I wondered if this would be a difficult moment for me—I'm not with my former colleagues for what would have been my final swearing in. But I'm delighted to be here to show my support for Marcia.

Soon, I'm transported back to my own first swearing-in.

* * * *

On January 10, 2007, at the age of 60, I was officially sworn in as state representative of the 91st District. It had been a long time since I had experienced such pure, unabated excitement. I was nervous, but I simply couldn't stop smiling. Nor could I keep my heart from pounding. Would I be able to say everything I was supposed to say? Would I perform my swearing-in duties correctly? Would I flub my lines in front of all these people on my first day? Anything was possible.

It helped to keep busy. Several cars full of supporters, friends, and family had driven to the capital, and we had planned a small reception for these guests in my new office, following the swearing-in.

One of my first decisions as representative-elect was to hire Chris Kilgroe as a staffer. He helped me go through the piles of resumes on my desk for the second staffer. After interviewing several applicants, I decided on Melissa Weipert, a bright and talented woman who was not only a huge asset to our staff, but became a friend as well. Chris and Melissa put on the finishing touches for the reception—straightening the office and laying out food for our guests: chicken salad sandwiches, sweet pickles, chocolate chip cookies, and soft drinks.

Our cell phones were abuzz—we were trying to make sure everybody knew where to go in the Capitol Building and how to find their tickets. As noon approached, I left the office, took the elevator down 11 floors, walked through the lobby, across the street, and up the front stairs of the capitol—the same time-worn wooden steps senators and governors had been using since the building was completed in 1878. For more than a century, Michigan's decision makers had walked up these steps to their swearing-in ceremonies.

That day, every inch of the capitol was jam-packed with people from around the state: well-wishers, friends, and families of those about to take the official step of becoming state legislators. I had fretted about getting good tickets so our guests could see the ceremony—either from the gallery or on the TV in the Appropriations Room. I hoped I had succeeded. There were so many people!

For some reason, the person I remember most vividly from the crush of attendees at the capitol that day is Lorraine Finley. While working on a campaign, people are usually in their everyday casual clothes, but today everyone was gussied up, including Lorraine. Her brown hair was nicely poufed; she was wearing a lacy dress with a dark skirt and greeted me with a wide smile and a hug. Lorraine was such a steadfast, loyal friend and campaign worker. She had come to headquarters every week of the campaign and was 100% dependable. She's a perfect example of the many wonderful people on whom I came to depend during my campaign. It was so appropriate to have her at the swearing-in.

I fought through the crowds to the chamber and took my seat. On that day, we didn't have our own seats because we weren't yet officially state representatives. We were seated, not according to parties, as is normal, but according to our districts. The front right of the chamber was occupied by the Detroit delegation, the back left by the Upper Peninsula delegation. Everyone in between was seated numerically, in order of state districts.

I took my seat, feeling the great history of this day—and my place in it—from my fingertips to my toes. For more than 150 years, Michigan legislators had taken the step I was about to take. I could feel the presence of past leaders in the chamber.

Finally, when everyone was seated, Majority Floor Leader Steve Tobocman began the proceedings. His voice echoed through the chamber, and the sound of it took me back to the day in August 2006 when Steve had come to Muskegon to knock on doors for my campaign. After knocking for hours, he had stayed late and helped my team mail out information to absentee voters. It was one of those nights on the campaign when we were working late and getting slap-happy.

My son Shawn, my husband Phil and I on the
day of our official swearing-in.

Steve had rolled up his sleeves and joined in. But now there
he stood, far from that night and those campaign memories,
in his role as one of the most powerful people in the state.

We stood en masse, raised our right hands, and said our
oaths. Suddenly, we were official state representatives of
Michigan! It was a moment I had never fully imagined.
Actually, each of us had experienced a less ceremonial,
official swearing-in at some point between Election Day and
the first day of January. But the day I stood with my fellow
elected representatives was the day when my new title finally
seemed real.

After the swearing-in, we chose our seats in the chamber,
another long-held tradition of the House. At the front of the
chamber, where the clerks sat, our names had been put in a
large, circular wire basket, which turned, much like a Bingo

basket. A young person on the front podium pulled out one name at a time and gave it to the clerk, who announced it. When we heard our name, each of us called out our desired seat number. When all the names had been called and the seats chosen, all 110 of us representatives picked up our coats and purses, man bags and briefcases, and took them to our new seats. Pandemonium broke out in the chamber as we laughed, talked, and settled in, giddy with excitement— the Democrats on the left and the Republicans on the right, as is the custom.

My first-term seatmate was Doug Bennett, from the 92nd District, also in Muskegon County. Doug was—and still is—a strong advocate of working men and women. He never let any of his fellow Democrats forget how hard people work to earn their pay and their benefits. He also had a great sense of humor and always cut right to the issue at hand. He couldn't have been a better seatmate. Sometimes he gave me a hard time about how I parked my car in the staff parking lot behind the Capitol Building, complaining that I parked so sloppily that it interfered with his space, next to mine. There's no doubt in my mind that I deserved that teasing. No matter how hard I tried, though, I simply couldn't get my car straight into that parking spot. The space was ample; it was purely operator error that caused the problem. It usually took me two or three tries.

Representative Kate Ebli from Monroe sat behind me, and Representative Terry Brown, from the thumb of Michigan (and the first Democrat elected in his district for more than 100 years), sat in front of me. Representative Steve Lindbergh, from the Upper Peninsula, sat across the aisle near others from the U.P.; I became an honorary member of the U.P. delegation. Steve was one of the first people I met when I arrived in Lansing—we had been in the same grad program at Northern Michigan University 30 years earlier. Representative Marie Donigan, from Royal Oak, who became a good friend, and who was (and still is) a tireless advocate for public transportation, sat in front of Steve.

Through all the ups and downs of that first year serving the people of Michigan, including the all-night sessions and the difficult decisions, when all eyes in the state were on us—these were the people who stood with me. It was a unique and inexplicable experience and formed friendships for life.

But back to my swearing-in and to the beginning of my new life in politics.

My family was with me, along with many other families sitting in the chamber with a loved one who was about to be sworn into office. Sharing this day with my husband, Phil, and our adult children, Robin and Phil, was pure joy.

After taking our official chamber seats, the House formally elected Andy Dillon to the role of House Speaker. Andy Dillon spoke eloquently on that swearing-in day; his words were inspiring and heartfelt. It felt to me like a glorious new day in Lansing. Finally, Democrats had the gavel and our agenda would prevail—or so we thought on that bright, fresh afternoon.

After the ceremony, my friends and family walked across the capitol lawn to my office on the 11th floor of the Cora Anderson House Office Building (HOB). It was always a thrill to show people my magnificent office, with a large window overlooking the capitol (as all the representatives' offices had).

"The desk alone is bigger than any office I ever had as a speech therapist in the public schools," was my standard line. I said it because it seemed ridiculous to me that legislators are treated like royalty while students who need speech services work in unheated closets and empty storerooms.

In fact, all the offices and committee rooms in the Cora Anderson HOB were stately and impressive. I was somewhat embarrassed about having such an office at a time when so many in our state were struggling to put food on the table. The building was constructed in the 1990s, when Michigan's economy was flush. It never ceases to amaze me that so many of our Republican legislators are willing to cut funds for school children without a second thought, but are perfectly willing to pay for such an elaborate building for themselves.

One thing I cherish about my swearing-in day was the fact that my dear cousin, Katie Bryant, was able to attend. Katie had led the way for me into the field of speech therapy. She was an only child, and so became the sixth child in the Hostetler family. Katie also shared with me a love of politics and was thrilled to be part of the ceremony. Within the year, we lost Katie to a quick and deadly form of leukemia. My swearing-in day was one of the last times I saw her alive— making that day an even more precious memory.

Later that afternoon, when most of the guests had gone home, I escorted a few close friends and family members to the Capitol Building to show them the chamber and the caucus room, where I would be spending so much of my time in the coming term. When my daughter, Robin, noticed people praising and flattering me and rushing to open doors for me, she told me flat-out that my family wasn't going to allow my new job to go to my head. She, along with the rest of my family, kept their word. They kept me humble. Not that the day-to-day frustrations of being a state representative in a state losing jobs and citizens in droves wasn't enough to keep me humble—but my family wanted to be sure. In the coming years, they also would do everything they could to protect me from the nastiness that is an inescapable part of being a public servant in this day and age.

After that tour of the chamber, we gathered for a meal at Clara's, a restaurant in an old train station on Michigan Avenue a few blocks from the capitol. We talked and laughed for hours. It was a wonderful, unforgettable evening, with the stresses of the campaign behind us and the responsibilities of governing ahead of us.

Soon enough, we would be facing endless challenges, including the bane of every politician's existence—the media.

Chapter XI

Ink By the Barrel

I'm at my table in the coffee shop—the best place for letting my thoughts and feelings spill out onto the page. Again a fierce storm is howling outside—a good analogy for the anger I still hold toward the local media. I want and need to get to a place of peace as quickly as I can. I'm weary of holding onto burdensome grudges. But problems with the present-day media continue.

A recent Michigan law puts an "emergency manager" in charge of struggling communities and school systems, giving the manager nearly complete decision-making power—with carte blanche from the state and no local input. Michigan state leaders seem indifferent to the need to find ways to help communities and school districts overcome fiscal challenges while maintaining the principles of a democratic society. It's far easier for them to throw democracy out the window, which is what the current legislature has done.

The media has allowed this by failing to ask the tough questions. The news is tied up with a bright bow and delivered to the readership without the gritty details that might make advertisers uncomfortable.

I'm frustrated now, as I was frustrated then.

While complaining about the media may read like sour grapes, not discussing it at all—or not giving my honest thoughts about it—seems phony. So for better or worse, I'm diving into a discussion about how I saw the media, as both a candidate and a public official.

* * * *

I grew up in a newspaper family, so I know from firsthand experience that advertisers keep the media afloat. When merchants fail to advertise in newspapers or radio and TV stations, those media outlets take a financial nosedive. Although I understand this reality, I also believe that democracy won't survive if citizens can't learn the truth. This is why our founders made sure the U.S. Constitution included freedom of the press. Too often, though, advertisers determine editorial content—and when they do, uncomfortable truths remain hidden.

When I started in politics, I was naïve about the media's ability to influence voters. Information sources have incredible power and can use it carelessly. In choosing what to cover, what *not* to cover, and how to present the news, they sometimes twist the truth.

There must be a solution. Maybe it's as simple as media owners, editors, and reporters having more courage. In the meantime, I can't say I'm sorry my love/hate relationship with the local print media is over.

The first time I realized I wouldn't always be able to count on the *Muskegon Chronicle* (the local daily) for fair treatment was when I first announced my campaign, back in 2006. My team and I had spent weeks developing the perfect spot for the announcement: in front of the closed Saapi Paper Mill, to draw attention to Michigan's jobs crisis. We invited everyone we knew, because we wanted a crowd. Dan Farrough, Democratic House Press Secretary, drove over from Lansing before

Citizen Mary

the event and sat with me in my living room, coaching me on
how to deal with the press. He grilled me until I was ready for
any questions the media might throw at me. Sixty people
came out for the event—an unheard-of number for such an
event in Muskegon at that time.

I doubt that Holly Hughes, who made her announcement
for the same seat a few months after I was elected, had a
similar crowd when she announced her candidacy. Yet she
received coverage unlike anything I ever received in the
Chronicle: two separate articles and many photographs
spread across the front page—above the fold, below the fold,
and onto the second page—where the article stretched on for
what seemed like forever.

So what coverage did the *Chronicle* give me on that spring
day in 2006? None. Zilch. Nada. Zip. Not one darn word.
They told my campaign they didn't cover political campaign
announcements. The *White Lake Beacon* (the weekly newspaper in the White Lake area) at least gave me a small article on
the last page of their newspaper. But the *Muskegon Chronicle*? Nothing.

They claimed Holly's story was newsworthy because she
was at that time the national committeewoman for the
Republican Party. I guess they didn't think they could make
a story out of a lowly speech pathologist who had spent 30
years of her life in public schools giving children the precious
gift of communication before deciding to run for office. No
story there.

And when the *Chronicle* finally figured out that I was a
real, viable candidate, running a real campaign, did they call
my headquarters and ask to talk to me? No. Did they call
anyone who knew me? Not on your life. Instead, they went to
a well-known political reporter and commentator in Lansing
named Bill Ballenger. I had never met Republican Bill Bal-

lenger—had never even talked to him. He knew nothing about me. But apparently, he knew enough to know I was a "liberal." So that's what the *Chronicle* reported via a quote from Ballenger:

"On the other hand, Valentine, a political newcomer, is being perceived as being quite liberal—perhaps too much so for some voters in the district," Ballenger said.[11] And the caption under my picture read: *Valentine (D): Newcomer seen as quite liberal.*

At that point, I had been making calls to voters for months to talk with them about the issues. I didn't label myself, but simply talked about the issues that were important to them. Voters never dismissed me as a liberal when they learned what I was about. But once the *Chronicle* started using this label, I had a harder time with people who had strong feelings about voting for someone labeled "liberal." I started hearing remarks like, "I would never vote for you. You're a liberal. The *Chronicle* said so." Even the Republican reporter, Steve Gunn, commented in surprise, after he interviewed me, that I was more moderate than he had expected.

I have to admit, though, that the *Muskegon Chronicle* covered some stories about my influential opponent that didn't show him in a good light—which could have created difficulties for the newspaper. First, they put a story on the front page about a lawsuit brought against Farhat for cheating the widow of Joe Byerle—a prominent local war hero. Later, they covered another story that described Farhat's legal challenges related to taxes.

As the election neared, Steve Gunn did a story on each candidate, interviewing both me, and my opponent, for two

---

[11] *Muskegon Chronicle*, September 8, 2006, front page.

separate articles, and including our positions on many issues. That coverage was fair, and I appreciated it.

And then, perhaps because of those earlier stories about the incumbent, the *Muskegon Chronicle* surprised me. They endorsed me for state representative of the 91st District. The endorsement actually said that Muskegon should turn Election Day into "Valentine's Day." Very nice.

After the election, though, Steve Gunn seemed at times to slant his reporting about my work in office to hurt me politically. For instance, I can't remember any representative in my district working as hard as I did—I held monthly town hall meetings and coffee hours, answered all my e-mail, and provided extensive constituent services. Constantly researching bills and educating myself on the issues, I worked day and night and had no compunction about working across the aisle. Steve Gunn, however, wrote an article about me that portrayed me as lazy. Lazy! Somehow, he took a quote out of context and conjured up examples to support his point by talking to Republicans in Lansing, who would have loved nothing better than to put this seat back into Republican hands. Based on those partisan comments, he wrote a ridiculous article about me not having a good work ethic.

The article actually made it into the online version of the *Muskegon Chronicle*. The editor, Paul Keep, pulled it off quickly when he became aware of it, claiming it was posted there by accident. I always worried, though, about that article re-emerging in the hard copy of the *Muskegon Chronicle*.

Later, I had a discussion with Paul Keep about it.

"It's hard enough to be a citizen legislator, without having to fight the newspaper as well," I told him.

He heard me out. "You shouldn't have to fight the newspaper," he agreed. Thank you, Mr. Keep.

The sad truth is that readers often believe distorted articles like the one about my work ethic. So it's important to be vigilant, and object when something is inaccurate or unfair. But this takes enormous energy away from the important work that needs to be accomplished—energy better spent researching issues and solving constituents' concerns.

I would like to add here that the *Chronicle* was always gracious about allowing me to write a letter to the editor to get my point of view to readers if I disagreed with something, which I often did. But this was not nearly as powerful as a headline or a lead story would have been.

I would have to say that during my entire time in politics, I never had much success working with newspapers. They seemed to have defensiveness built into their DNA. For instance, whenever we passed an important piece of legislation through the House of Representatives, our writers sent press releases to the newspapers. All of the other state representatives with whom I worked saw those articles printed in their local newspapers from time to time. The *Chronicle*, however, never printed one of mine—not even one—in my four years as a representative. In fact, I was the only representative I could find who never had one of those press releases printed in my local daily. When I mentioned this fact to Paul Keep, he brushed me off by saying he simply didn't believe me.

Actually, the only time they ever referred to one of my press releases about legislation was when they used it to criticize me. One editorial writer (someone I have deep respect for) referred to me as "crowing" about the smoking ban bill we passed through the House of Representatives. He didn't like our bill because it left out the casinos. Sadly, that's sometimes the way democracy works. Good ideas take a while to work their way into law. When the bill finally passed during my second term, a compromise helped get it through. Smoking was allowed in casinos—but only on the gaming floor.

Interestingly, the *Chronicle* wrote articles about my successor, multi-millionaire Holly Hughes, three times within the first month—before she even had a chance to accomplish anything. When she was eventually defeated in the election of 2012, they printed a long, two-part article about her. I can't help but assume the *Chronicle* didn't want to get on the wrong side of all that money.

Early in my second term, Steve Gunn, whom I've already mentioned—a staunchly Republican political writer —retired. It was one of the happiest days of my political career. Succeeding him was Dave Alexander—smart, professional, and accurate. Another new reporter was Eric Gaertner. When Eric and Dave reported on meetings or forums, the articles, it seemed to me, reflected what actually had happened.

Eric Gaertner, the *Chronicle* writer, did an excellent job of providing good information to readers about one issue that came up during my second term. Teri Lynn Land, the Republican Secretary of State, decided to close a branch office in Whitehall, which is in my district. She actually closed 11 branches in the state, and ten of them were in the districts of Democratic representatives. These closings hurt families and saved the state little money. She had concocted the weirdest plan you could imagine: Close the branch office in the northern part of the county (in Whitehall) and the branch office located in central Muskegon County, and instead open one branch in the far southern part of the county (right next to Ottawa County, just south of us). This would have made access difficult for almost all Muskegon County residents while actually improving access for Ottawa County residents (who were already well covered and would have remained so under her plan). It was pretty obvious that she was going overboard to please the exceedingly Republican Ottawa County, while slapping the face of the Democratic Muskegon County. Blessedly, she eventually reversed herself on closing the centrally located branch, and gave up the nonsense about opening a branch office inches from the county line. She never wavered in closing the Whitehall Branch Office, though.

When news of the closings emerged, Representative Doug Bennett, 92nd District, and I, along with our staffs, went into action to find a way to keep that Whitehall office open. We tried petitions, town hall meetings, protests, letters to the editor, and legislation—everything we could think of to stop the closure of the Whitehall Branch Office. No one gained by this closure. I worked with Republicans and Democrats— anyone I could find to help provide a necessary service for our constituents. To this day, I see no sense in the White Lake Branch Office closure.

But in the end, Terri Lyn Land closed it, inconveniencing the citizens of this state—her constituents and mine—for no good reason. You can call it fiscal conservatism if you'd like. The truth is that losing the branch office has cost more than it saved. Now people must drive many miles for a service that was once close at hand.

Coincidentally, I later gathered signatures for a petition at the Apple Avenue Secretary of State's Office. I can't even begin to tell you the number of people lamenting the closure of the Whitehall branch and how frustrating it was to be down to one branch in our county. This is often the result of "fiscal conservatism"—pound wise and penny foolish. Thank you, Ms. Land.

Throughout the entire ordeal, though, I could count on Eric Gaertner and the *Chronicle* to provide substantial and accurate information to the public. That felt good. But then leadership at the *Chronicle* changed hands, and in my opinion, fair press coverage suffered. The final straw in my dealings with the *Chronicle* was during my Senate race. That was when I cancelled my subscription, once and for all—the first time in my six decades on this earth I haven't subscribed to a local daily. My opponent's party had been bashing me for weeks and had sent out nasty literature about me almost daily (I believe it was 18 pieces in all). Then Goeff Hansen began lying about me. The first time was at a public forum at West Shore Community College in Mason County. He said I wanted to put people's water under the complete control of the state. When I tried to correct that lie, the moderator threatened to turn my microphone off.

Then he was featured in a TV ad repeating the same lie— that I wanted the state to have complete control over peoples' water. Mr. Hansen's defenders like to say that he didn't lie personally—it was his party. But he stood right there in that ad and said it himself, though it simply wasn't true. I'm sure the ad polled well, which is why it was on the air endlessly. The Republican Party sent out endless nasty mailers, robo calls, radio ads, and TV spots that misrepresented me. After the election, it came out that they had spent a million dollars.

During this terrible campaign, Goeff Hansen actually sued me. It was a ridiculous issue related to a large yard sign with two extra letters on it (which I will explain in greater depth later in the book). Yup. This guy, who sold himself as a fiscal conservative wasted precious court time and taxpayer money to publicly humiliate me and win political points.

Geoff Hansen's campaign was the dirtiest I've ever seen— and I've been watching campaigns for a long time. He wouldn't even renounce a mailer the Chamber of Commerce sent out on his behalf in which my head was sticking out of a drain right next to a toilet with a plunger over my head. It read, "Send Mary Valentine down the drain." Yup. You heard right. Send Mary Valentine down the drain. That ad spoke volumes about how low the Chamber of Commerce was willing to go to defeat me. And Goeff Hansen was more than willing to put up with it.

Soon after this, the *Chronicle* endorsed Hansen. In doing so, in my view, they endorsed the dirtiest campaign many people had ever seen.

The *Chronicle* was one of the media I dealt with, but other media also made my job interesting. Rick Albin was a TV interviewer with whom I had always enjoyed talking. He wanted information and didn't seem interested in "gotcha" journalism. From time to time, I was a guest on his Sunday morning television show, "To the Point." Usually, I was the only woman being interviewed, along with some of my male colleagues in the legislature. That's why I suggested a show with women politicians: two Democrats and two Republicans. Rick liked my idea and soon after, on a cold winter morning, he interviewed four Michigan women politicians. I was excited and hoped some young women would be watching so they would see that women can, and do, govern along with men.

Tim Skubick, moderator of Friday night's show, "Off the Record," has a different interviewing style than Rick Albin. An experienced interviewer who has been covering Lansing news for decades, Tim isn't shy when interviewing politicians, often trying to trap them into saying something stupid and politically risky. He frequently succeeds.

I admire Tim and enjoy his columns—he's a smart man and an excellent writer. But that little girl inside me who could barely talk as a child was always warning me not to let myself be cornered into saying something that could be used against me in a campaign. I knew my success depended on this mindfulness. So Tim's was one show I had no interest in doing.

Once I almost got caught in his web. He was lying in wait for me outside the Education Committee room when the controversial Race to the Top legislation was coming up for a vote. The bill faced possible opposition from teachers' unions. Because I was a former teacher, Mr. Skubick thought he could trap me into saying something that would make a juicy quote for him or trick me into saying something I would later regret. What happened was quite the opposite.

The committee room was packed to overflowing; many people were milling about outside. Both print and television news media were present. When I passed through the door of the committee room, Tim Skubick caught me by surprise. He stood inches away from me, stuck the microphone into my face and pounced.

"You're a former teacher. What do you think of the Race to the Top legislation?" he asked.

Fortunately, my wits were with me that day. "I am on the side of a good, strong education system," I answered.

"What do you mean by stronger?" he pressed.

"I didn't say stronger," I replied. "*You* said stronger."

He walked away, disappointed. My response was never mentioned. If I had blurted out something more controversial, I guarantee he would have reported it. He never approached me again.

Another reporter who circled our sessions endlessly was Peter Luke, a 25-year veteran correspondent for Booth Newspapers (which owned several Michigan newspapers). For most of that time, he wrote a column on budget, tax, and economic development policy issues. I noticed that his stories were usually dead-on accurate and contained thoughtful analysis. Although Luke no longer works for Booth Newspapers, he is still writing about Michigan in a weekly column in the *Bridge Magazine*.

Radio also was part of the media scene. Sometimes when I was out knocking doors, I got calls from headquarters. "So-and-so from National Public Radio (NPR) would like to interview you about the water bill," my staffer would say. "Do you want to take the call?"

Or "Someone from NPR would like to interview you about the education budget. Can you call her back?"

I loved being asked my opinion and always was glad to cooperate. Although I never completely got rid of the butterflies in my tummy during interviews, they did flutter less the longer I was in office. Early on, I developed a survival strategy to get me through. My goal was simple: Prepare for the interview carefully, don't worry, and get out alive. I also had a policy of never watching or listening to my own interviews after I was finished. They couldn't have been too bad, though—I received many compliments on my thoughtful responses.

All in all, I believe the most important thing to remember about media and politics is this: Read any news about any political candidate with a big grain of salt. And do your own research about candidates from a range of sources.

Chapter XII

A Day in the Life...

Although losing the election was, of course, a deep disappointment, every cloud, as they say, has its silver lining. The silver lining of my new life is sleeping in late whenever I choose. I sometimes wish I could be part of the current fight in Lansing, but not on those dark winter days when I can stay snuggled in bed until I feel like getting up. I never had that choice while serving as a legislator. I especially remember some of those cold winter mornings when we were in session.

* * * *

It was a dark, cold February, and morning had come way too early. But legislative work was calling my name, so I hopped out of bed, fixed my hair, brushed my teeth, grabbed my phone, bundled up, and headed out the door for a drive to Lansing. I actually liked driving on those dark mornings. When the sun popped over the horizon, it usually nearly blinded me—even if I lowered the visor, put on sunglasses, and wore a brimmed hat. Dark mornings were a welcome relief from that blinding sun as I headed east from Muskegon to Lansing.

After about a zillion trips to Lansing I had my landmarks figured out quite well. When I got to the first rest stop, I was 20 minutes out. The second rest stop meant I was almost there. Soon I would be pulling into my own parking spot behind the capitol. From there, I would tighten my scarf around my neck and head off across the lawn and into the House Office Building. I once heard that the capitol lawn was the coldest place in Michigan, because the bridge connecting the two towers of the House Office Building created a wind tunnel that made the walk across the street unbearably frigid.

On the coldest mornings, I would rush into the closest door, which took me straight into the State Plate—a small cafeteria that had breakfast and lunch available for all who worked at the House Office Building. Some mornings, I would stop to say hi to Mark Brewer, then chair of Michigan's Democratic Party, drinking his morning coffee and keeping his eye on things while perusing the *Lansing Journal*. I often would spot several of my colleagues, along with a handful of lobbyists, deep in conversation. From the State Plate, I would jump on the elevator for the ride up to my office on the eleventh floor. Typically, people riding the elevator were congenial—happy to chat about the news of the day. Partisanship didn't exist on the elevator—just friendly greetings.

"Have you heard how long session will be today?"

"I think the agenda is short and we'll get out early."

"I'll be glad when the budgets are finally done."

When I first got to Lansing, I had several embarrassing elevator moments, because I couldn't always remember the names and faces of people who had helped me get elected (despite my eternal gratitude). Once I introduced myself to a staffer in the elevator and she replied, "I know you, Mary. I knocked doors for you last summer."

"Well, thank you so much for your help," I finished sheepishly.

But sometimes, wonderful exchanges took place on the elevator. My favorite story concerns Dennis Kawthorn of the venerable Kelly/Kawthorn lobbying firm, one of the most prestigious in Lansing. Although I bumped into lobbyists from the firm frequently, I never actually saw Kelly or Kawthorn. They were starting to seem like phantom lobbyists to me. During my second term, when the Democrats were looking for a great candidate for governor, I read something in the *Muskegon Chronicle* about Dennis Kawthorn. It was a letter to the editor from a former student of his who raved about what a wonderful man he was, and even suggested he should run for governor.

The day after I read that letter, I entered the elevator to see an older gentleman standing there whom I had never met before. As usual, I introduced myself. He replied, "I'm Dennis Kawthorn."

I couldn't believe my ears. As I picked up my jaw from the floor, I managed to respond: "I just read the most flattering letter to the editor about you in the *Muskegon Chronicle*."

"Really?" He said. "Who wrote it?"

"Can't remember the name, but it was from a former student of yours. It was in yesterday's paper; you should be able to find it."

The next time I got on the elevator, I met a Kelly/Kawthorn lobbyist who told me that Dennis Kawthorn was quite proud of that letter. He had found it in the *Chronicle*, copied it, posted it on the office bulletin board, and sent copies out to everyone in the firm. I was glad to have brought it to his attention.

That is so Lansing. The five or so blocks in downtown Lansing are like a small town. Everyone knows each other and rumors fly like the wind. It takes only a few minutes for every staffer, legislator, and lobbyist in town to hear any new rumor.

Legislators need to absorb an enormous amount of information to understand the issues they will be voting on: the ins and outs of school funding, the importance of keeping the public school system strong, the ongoing need for public transportation, and the reality of how public service closings might affect constituents. Add to that the dangers and challenges of working in our prisons, the impact of farming on our state's economy, and the regulation of gun ownership—the list goes on and on. In these times of term limits for Michigan's elected officials, those interested in advocating for a particular issue have the daunting job of educating a new batch of legislators every other year. It's a non-stop job, with legislators continuously coming and going with each election cycle.[12]

A common forum for conveying information was a breakfast meeting—usually held at the Radisson Hotel in downtown Lansing. The reasoning behind breakfast meetings, I believe, is that the best way to grab legislators' attention is to offer them food—and along with that food, a quick round of much-needed information. Typically, the breakfast was self-serve: steaming pans of eggs, bacon, and pancakes. I often took a muffin and fruit of some sort (but I must admit that I sometimes was tempted by the French toast or pancakes). And always, in the morning, we drank endless coffee. After filling up my plate, I would wander into a room filled with round tables, sit down, and hear about various issues while I ate. The program typically included an introduction of all the

---

[12] This is another good reason for Michigan to repeal its legislative term limits, which are currently crippling our legislature.

legislators present. Late arrivals were introduced as they entered.

Afterward, I would hurry the few blocks back to the House Office Building, where I would begin my day answering e-mails, letters, and phone calls. My excellent staff took care of many details of this correspondence for me, but I often responded as well. Sometimes, lobbyists or visitors from the district came to my office to update me on various issues. I especially remember a group of young people who visited me from Muskegon's Webster House, a place for youth in crisis. All of them had already experienced huge challenges in their young lives, but were now on the right track—and rightfully proud of themselves. On this occasion, they were asking for more funding for Webster House. I was always thrilled to see young people advocating for issues important to them and becoming acquainted with how our democracy works. After listening to their concerns, I pointed out to them the Capitol Building, directly across the street. They took pictures and several shared their survival stories with me. I was deeply touched. Webster House is a people redeemer—worth every penny we invest there.

Then it was off to committee meetings. I always had thought of a committee as a small group of people around a table, hashing out details and making joint decisions. But legislative committees don't resemble that scenario one iota. Instead, legislators sit in large black swivel chairs at long wooden benches—much like judges' benches, but long enough to accommodate from 10 to 20 legislators. Each legislator has access to a microphone (a flexible wire tube with a small black speaker at the end), which he or she turns on before speaking, and a laptop. The committee chair sits at the center, right next to a clerk whose job is to help the chair follow House rules. The minority co-chair sits beside the clerk, and the majority co-chair sits either next to the chair, or next to the policy person assigned to that committee. The chair has a huge gavel and can turn off the members' mikes if they're out of line. I'm happy to say that in my two terms I don't remember a single time that a committee chair turned off a mike to silence a legislator. (I am equally unhappy to report that in the legislature following mine, from what I've heard, chairs sometimes used, or threatened to use, the tactic of silencing legislators.)

The chair would gavel the meeting to order, call the roll, and take motions to accept the minutes of the previous meeting. In committee, no one talked unless the chair called on him or her. It was all extremely formal: A legislator who wanted to speak alerted the clerk, who would write down the legislator's name, to be called on in order. The person whose turn it was to speak could say only one thing, or ask one question, and then would have to ask the chair for permission to make an additional statement or ask a further question.

By law, all committee meetings are open to the public. And I encourage everyone to occasionally attend a legislative committee meeting. If the door of the committee room is closed, open it and go in. People always wander in and out during committee meetings. Anyone can testify: Just fill out a card with your name, organization, and whether you're for or against the legislation being discussed. Visitors to the committee can fill out the card whether or not they want to speak. But if someone wants to say something, the chair is supposed to provide that opportunity. The person—or people—testifying sit at a long table facing the legislators, with a microphone or two. Screens are available for slide presentations and plenty of seats for guests. After each presentation, legislators normally ask questions or make comments. Before the end of the meeting, all the cards are read into the record.

Initially, the formality of the whole thing intimidated me. I didn't want to say something that would make me look stupid. I soon learned this wasn't a problem during one of my first Education Committee meetings, when a woman made a presentation highlighting the necessity of early childhood education. Her presentation was accurate and thorough, stressing the importance of a strong early childhood education to enable young people to be successful in school. A Republican representative then asked a question that revealed a rather shallow understanding of the issue.

"Don't you think mothers can raise their own children?" he asked.

The woman was so dumbfounded by the question she couldn't even answer it.

That was the first time I spoke up in committee.

"Early childhood programs are not babysitting," I explained. "These programs offer age-appropriate curriculum to prepare students for kindergarten. The program kick-starts a child's educational career so it will be successful. But parents still raise their own children."

I could say this with some certainty because I was familiar with the Perry Preschool Project of the late sixties, which tracked the success of preschool programs aimed at children living in poverty. The study followed a group of students from early childhood into their forties; it provided clear evidence that for every dollar spent on high-quality early childhood education programs, seventeen dollars is saved in the long run.[13]

---

[13] In addition, I had my own memories to draw on. I started kindergarten in 1951, and I *still* remember the kids in my

Most of the time, a committee room contains a few interested people and a handful of lobbyists along with the legislators. But when a controversial topic comes up, the room might become jam-packed with those advocating for and against the legislation being discussed. That's the way it was when we struggled with the out-of-state trash issue, as well as the issue of the absolute immunity that drug companies have in the state of Michigan—even when their drugs harm or kill.

In fact, Michigan is the only state in the nation that gives complete immunity to drug companies. Basically, Michigan citizens have been stripped of their right to hold drug companies accountable. The initial purpose of this law was to bring more pharmaceutical companies to Michigan. Although drug companies didn't come in droves and some that were here left despite this law, the law has remained on the books. Citizens continue to be harmed by it, because pharmaceutical companies shrug off citizens who are damaged by their product. The drug companies know that in Michigan, citizens' hands are tied. In my experience, people are appalled when they learn about this law. Nonetheless, the Republican legislature strongly supports it. When we Democrats were in the majority in the House of Representatives, we tried to change it. But the Republican Senate stopped us cold.

And then there's the trash. Garbage pours into our state continuously—from Canada, neighboring states, and be-

---

class who had attended what they called at the time "nursery school." They were miles ahead of the rest of us on the first day of school—an advantage that continued through high school graduation, and into life. I personally believe that all students need and deserve early childhood programs to better ensure success. But of course, parents still raise their own children.

yond—some even as far away as Florida. The reason other states send their trash to Michigan is because we charge so little.[14] This low charge means we are paying for road and bridge repairs strictly with tax dollars. Further, this out-of-state trash is likely contaminating our water supply. When Pennsylvania had a similar problem, they increased the dumping charge to a reasonable rate, and the problem was solved. In Michigan, the Democrats were in favor of a similar solution, which would have cost citizens about a dollar a month. But again, the Republican Senate wouldn't budge, so out-of-state trash continues to pour into Michigan. I had taken a strong stand on both these issues during my campaign, and I was terribly disappointed that these bills, which I felt were so important, would languish and die in the Republican Senate.

Committee meetings usually lasted anywhere from a half hour to an hour and a half. The chair then would pound his or her gavel to adjourn the meeting. After the meeting, I often walked the six floors up to my office to squeeze in a little exercise. Back in my office, I would relish a hot cup of coffee before I dove into the mountain of work waiting for me: contacts from constituents, research to complete on bills we'd be voting on, and preparation for bills that I wanted to introduce. I always had too much to do—and most of it was due yesterday.

---

[14] According to a January 18, 2011, MLive.com article by Jeff T. Wattric, our state's "tipping fee" is 21 cents per ton of garbage dumped, while other states charge significantly more—even up to $13 a ton in Wisconsin. Another MLive writer, Melissa Anders, indicated in an article published on February 12, 2014, that about 17% of all waste in Michigan landfills comes from Canada, and another 6% comes from other states.

One of the strangest e-mails I ever received was from Cindy Larsen, president of Muskegon's Chamber of Commerce. It was a rant about how terrible state workers are: lazy, greedy, and always taking long vacations they hadn't earned and didn't deserve. One particular passage of this message still sticks in my memory: She called state workers "greedy money-grabbers." Yup. That was her language. The president of our Chamber of Commerce thought this was a good thing to write in her e-mail about state workers.

My husband, Phil, was a state worker. He worked at the Department of Human Services (DHS) as an Assistance Payments worker for 25 years. I'd like to point out here that my husband never was able to take a long vacation, because his workload was far too heavy. Every family vacation was squeezed into five working days. Oh, he had vacation days— but if he took them, the work piled up to the point where he could never catch up. He literally was called back to work when he was at his mother's deathbed. So I'm not going to commiserate with anyone about long vacations and lazy, money-grabbing state workers.

I'm sorry to report that discrediting state workers is a strategy used by some to demean those workers and cut their pay. In fact, when I read that e-mail back in 2007, a slow boil started at the bottom of my feet and worked its way up. I am quite certain steam was rolling out of my ears by the time I got to the end of that letter. Even worse, Cindy Larsen had copied everyone on the Chamber of Commerce Board. It occurred to me that, if she really wanted everyone to know what she thought about state workers, she should send her thoughts out to the state workers themselves. So we helped her out with that and sent it to a few DHS workers as well as to some employees who risk their lives daily working in our state prisons. Cindy ended up with some fires to put out.

Apparently, she thought I owed her an apology. Maybe I did, but in my view she should have apologized to all state workers and their families, including my husband, for her insulting language.

But I digress.

Back to my day as a legislator: Next, it was off to session in the capitol. Lunch was first, though. Typically, several fundraisers are held during the lunch hour in Lansing. While lobbyists pay to attend these events, legislators receive endless complimentary invitations. Lobbyists have access to legislators during these lunches—enabling them to discuss pending issues and laws as well as build relationships. Those lunches are an important part of what happens in Lansing. They also are the reason most legislators gain weight while they are in office.

Often, groups—school associations, Public Health Department employees, or organizations like Fight Crime: Invest in Kids—came from around the state and held meetings at the Capitol Building during the lunch hour. These associations and groups wanted legislators to know what they were accomplishing in order to assure needed funding wouldn't dry up—and to inform us of their current needs. They would set up a buffet for legislators along with informational displays about their agendas. While we ate, we went over issues of concern.

Once I met with students from Mona Shores High School at a lunch-hour event in the Capitol Building. They were there with their principal, Jennifer Bustard, and I had an opportunity to see some of their science projects. It's always delightful for me to see students' work. I'm quite sure they were advocating for school funding. People were constantly asking us not to cut their funding—or to restore what had already been cut—during my years in the legislature. Since

I've left the legislature, school funding has been decimated, and the students are paying the price.

At another of those noon meetings, I met Susan Clotier-Meyer, Executive Director of the Disability Connection of West Michigan, located in Muskegon. She was (and I'm sure still is) a fierce advocate for public transportation. Her clientele are those who must depend on public transportation for their livelihood. She updated me about a proposal she was working on to bring more public transportation to Muskegon County and the surrounding area, and asked me to write a letter to advocate for it. I gladly agreed. This is just one example of what transpires during a typical lunch hour.

After lunch, it was off to session—a world of its own. Session started at 1:30 p.m. on Tuesdays and Wednesdays, and at noon on Thursdays. We always began with a prayer, led by a member, and the Pledge of Allegiance, led by the speaker pro-tem. All-night sessions were adjourned at midnight—then immediately re-opened with the pledge and a prayer once again.

All legislators' names are listed on an electric board at the front of the chamber—one board on the right and one on the left, so they can be seen easily from everywhere in the chamber. During session, when the board is turned on, all names appear in orange until that legislator casts a vote. Each legislator has a console at his or her seat, with voting buttons. If the legislator votes no, his or her name changes to red. A yes vote changes the name to green. Legislators sit at their own desks and are supplied with laptop computers. Miniature lectern-like platforms with microphones attached are sprinkled throughout the chamber. Any legislator who wants to make a floor speech stands at one of the microphones and raises a hand until the speaker pro-tem calls out his or her name and turns the mike on.

"Thank you, Mr. (or Madam) Speaker," is the opening response.

Then come the remarks, for instance: "I would like to introduce 39 students and four teachers from Beachwood Elementary School in Fruitport."

Or this: "I rise today in opposition to this bill."

Or: "I would like to offer an amendment to this bill."

Other legislators listen to floor speeches, but aren't supposed to cheer, clap—or even boo—at the speech's conclusion.

Generally, voting went smoothly during my time in the legislature; almost all bills were passed on a bipartisan basis. While I was serving, we made every attempt to meet as many needs as possible and make as many compromises as necessary to create a good, strong bill that was supported by most legislators. We were forced to compromise to get anything passed through both chambers, since one chamber had a Democratic majority and the other a Republican majority. This situation often resulted in bill swapping. We would pass one of theirs through the House, if they would pass one of ours through the Senate. It sounds juvenile, but it was a strategy to which we had to resort if we were to pass any of our bills. Sometimes, no matter how much compromising and conferring we did, issues remained intractable and agreement wasn't possible. In those cases, lots of hoopla and floor discussion ensued.

After I left the legislature in December 2010, the Republicans were in complete control of every branch of government: Secretary of State, Attorney General, the House of Representatives, the Senate, the Supreme Court, and the governorship. Compromise came to a screeching halt and Republicans made decisions unilaterally, without input from Democrats. Republicans love this state of affairs, of course, because it's so efficient. But it's not the way democratic governance is supposed to work, and much of the legislation is deeply flawed and shortsighted. Many in Lansing miss the days of good, healthy compromise in the interest of making good public policy for Michigan's citizens.

An excellent orator on our side of the aisle, whom I always appreciated and loved listening to, was Coleman Young, Jr., son of the venerable Detroit Mayor, Coleman Young. Coleman Young, Jr., though not an attorney, knows the Michigan Constitution backward and forward, and often referred to it during floor speeches—and even in caucus discussions.

One floor debate that stands out vividly in my memory took place after the worldwide economic collapse of 2008. The year before, Michigan had voted to restore a small amount of the income tax that had been cut to 3.9% by a previous legislature, so that our public schools, public safety agencies, and other institutions still could safely deliver services to Michigan citizens. During this debate, the Republican legislators waxed philosophical about how terrible it had been for the economy that we had earlier voted in this tiny income tax restoration.

I finally was compelled to stand and point out that the worldwide economic collapse didn't occur because of a small income tax increase in the state of Michigan!

"The last tax increase didn't have the intended effect," the Republicans repeated, one after the next.

"But it did have the intended effect," I countered. "It kept our schools open and our public safety strong!"

It was a pointless argument. The Republican talking point that day was that the tax increase hadn't had any positive effect, and had basically helped bring Michigan's economy to its current crisis. That was their talking point and they were sticking to it like glue.

When all the votes on the docket had been taken on a given session day and the majority floor leader had officially ended the meeting, legislators were free to go. Most packed up their belongings and left the building. The clerks then read new bills into the docket as the chamber cleared. I loved to stay in my seat after session. I enjoyed the stillness. I returned phone calls, answered e-mails, and researched upcoming legislation. And I marveled that I was a part of whatever had happened that day. When the chamber was quiet and empty, its intensity increased. I became profoundly aware that this where so much of Michigan's history occurred. Our constitution came to life here, along with Soapy Williams' dream of connecting our two peninsulas. Governor Milliken had started his career in this chamber. I breathed in the Michigan history that lingered in the air.

On Tuesday and Wednesday nights, various groups typically held receptions around town—many at Troppo's, a restaurant on the corner of Capital and Michigan, The Firm, a bar in downtown Lansing, or various lobbyists' offices.

Once a year, the Farm Bureau had a meeting at the Lansing Center. When a legislator walked in, they announced the name to the entire delegation to enable people to connect with their legislators. I especially liked the farmers who came to these receptions. They worked extraordinarily hard and were clear about their priorities—but at the same time were open to dialogue and compromise.

After attending a few receptions, my workday was over. I either headed for home, or stayed at the Residence Inn on Saginaw Road. Sometimes, at the end of a long day when I stayed in Lansing, I would stop for a big, juicy hamburger, a cold beer, and a session with the latest *USA Today* crossword puzzle.

Chapter XIII

Being There For the People of the 91st District

I cringe when I hear people say that all politicians are crooks. Certainly there are crooked politicians; I won't deny that. Yet, when we run into an incompetent doctor, do we say all doctors are incompetent? When a waitress forgets our coffee, do we disparage all waitresses? It bugs me when people take that position about their legislators. And when voters complain about legislators' lack of knowledge and experience? Come on, folks. When the people of Michigan voted in these ridiculously short term limits, they voted to have perennially inexperienced legislators. The voters created this situation; they should either stop complaining about it or change it.

Those who bash all legislators, though, clearly never met my friend and former colleague Brenda Clack, former State Representative from Flint. She's been on my mind today, as I struggle to stop berating myself because I lost the Senate race.

* * * *

I served with Brenda Clack during my first term in the legislature, when we both spent hour after hour in Lansing. Together we sat through afternoons of dead-end negotiations from our elected leaders. As the dinner hour approached, we would hear the gavel bang and Speaker Pro Tem Mike Sak would announce our dinner break.

Brenda Clack, Kathleen Law, Kate Ebli, Marie Donigan, and I often met for dinner. I got to know Brenda more intimately and came to respect her more deeply during the many hours we shared in restaurants around the capitol. Brenda probably doesn't even break five feet—but she has enough ethical standards for someone twice her size. She also is, without a doubt, one of the hardest-working women I've ever met—a politician who meant business and didn't waste one moment of her time in the legislature. An extremely sharp dresser, she always wore spiffy scarves that perfectly accented her colorful suits and stylish shoes. Her husband had held her seat in the House before her, but when she stepped in to fill that seat and represent the people of Flint, she made it clear she was her own woman—one who cared deeply about the people she served.

The next time you enter a restaurant in which no one is smoking, you can thank Brenda Clack. She never stopped pushing for smoke-free workplace legislation. In fact, she was working on it during her last night in the legislature. She left the chamber broken-hearted—at the last moment, the bill got stuck in legislative limbo with no time left for its passage. When we were miraculously able to pass that bill during my second term, she made the trip to Lansing and stood proudly beside Governor Granholm while the bill was signed.

When all is said and done, that is one law that I, too, am proud to have been part of passing. Lives have been saved—and will continue to be saved—because of that law.

Like me, Brenda was a former teacher. And having dedicated her life to children, she understood, at a personal level, the importance of equal education for all children. Many in the legislature (and Brenda was one of them) were concerned about homeschooled children. Although many parents do an incredible job educating their children at home (and in fact, I homeschooled my own son for a while and found it a positive experience for both of us), we increasingly hear of home-schooled students who actually don't get an education at all.

In recent years, many teachers have noticed an increasing number of students who get pulled out of school so their parents can "homeschool" them. A few years later, those students return to school, years behind their peers. Clearly, this is no advantage for these students—which should concern all of us, whether we send our children to public or private school, or choose to homeschool. Failing to educate the next generation affects everyone.

Another aspect of homeschooling that concerns me is the reality of children who are abused or neglected in their homes and have little contact with anyone outside of their families. It is often a caring teacher who recognizes the signs of abuse or neglect and alerts the proper authorities. I worry that some abusive parents might use the pretense of home-schooling to hide what's happening in their homes.

So Brenda Clark created a simple piece of legislation to require homeschooled students to be registered. The legislation wasn't an attempt to interfere with homeschooling parents, nor did it contain any provisions for forced instruction. It simply required students to register to become home-schooled. As a parent who homeschooled, I would have appreciated such a thing.

I was tempted to co-sponsor the bill when Brenda asked me to, but I also had some reservations about it. The bill could too easily be misconstrued, and I knew that co-sponsoring an innocuous-looking piece of legislation could create huge headaches for legislators. I suspected that

Brenda's bill would be unpopular among the homeschooling crowd, and also was well aware of the large number of homeschooled children in my district. I wasn't at all sure these families would understand the bill's intentions, so I declined to sign it.

It was a relatively innocuous bill, and because everyone thought so highly of Brenda, many of our colleagues co-sponsored it when Brenda approached them. So Brenda proceeded to introduce the bill. That was when all hell broke loose. The day after the bill was dropped, every homeschooling parent in the state of Michigan contacted every single one of the co-sponsors of that bill. The co-sponsors' phones were tied up. Their e-mail boxes were crammed full, and their mailboxes were filled with letters. Boy, were those homeschooling parents mad!

The proponents of homeschooling in Michigan launched a huge defense, with endless reasons why homeschooling is great for children. The assumption that Brenda's bill was an attack on homeschooling took hold, and war was declared. No stupid state legislators were going to deny concerned parents the privilege of homeschooling their precious children. On and on this went—for days. I was glad I hadn't co-sponsored this bill and put myself through all of that agony with my constituents.

The real point of this story, though, is to demonstrate the complex relationship between any legislator and his or her constituents. It's also a good example of the ways a bill's intentions can be lost to hyperbole. Brenda didn't want to interrupt anyone's homeschooling experience. She loved education, children, and families. But someone saw that bill, twisted its meaning to their own ends, then sent the twisted version to hundreds of people and got them hoppin' mad and ready to organize.

This unfortunate twisting of a bill's meaning is not uncommon. For instance, I always supported anti-bullying legislation and bills that attempted to put an end to hate crimes. Parents testified at length in Education Committee during both of my terms in favor of anti-bullying bills. Bullying is no laughing matter. Students die from bullying. Many of their parents came to the education committee and testified with stories that ripped our hearts out. In an April 5, 2012 article in Huff Post Katy Hall reported that according to the Gay, Lesbian and Straight Education Network, 9 out of 10 LGBT teens report being bullied at school and these students are two to three times more likely to commit suicide than their straight peers. Of course I voted yes on anti-bully legislation – both in committee and in the chamber. Anti-bullying measures can save lives.

The bill, of course, failed to pass in the Republican Senate during my term of office. Later, a greatly watered-down bill was passed into law. I stood firm on my objection to bullying for any reason, and always supported bills to penalize hate crimes.

Once, when I was knocking on doors in the village of Fruitport, I stopped at a little white house. The woman who answered was furious with me before I even could tell her who I was.

"You don't care if I get beat up!" she cried.

What? Of course I didn't want her to get beat up. I had no clue what she was talking about. Finally I pieced together her story—she was referring to some sort of hate crime or anti-bullying legislation that I had recently supported. An anti-gay group of which she was a member presented it to her like this: if she were beaten up for being a Christian, the perpetrator wouldn't pay a penalty—but gays would receive special protections if attacked, due to the bill I had supported. In fact, the bill clearly protected people from hate crimes or bullying because of religious affiliation as well—so obviously, what she was saying made no sense. I even sent her a copy of the bill to prove my point. I doubt if that particular woman changed her mind about me, though. She believed what she had been led to believe, regardless of the truth.

Other constituents were beyond wonderful about changing and improving their community through new legislation. For example, many folks in my district were outspoken supporters of animal rights. One such woman, April Auger, had become furious about a particularly vicious case of animal abuse she read about in the *Muskegon Chronicle* where the perpetrators got a slap on the wrist. She researched the current legislation and met with me at The Coffee House in Norton Shores. She had brought with her a copy of the current law, with the parts that she believed needed changing highlighted in yellow.

"We are letting these animal abusers off way too easy, Mary," she insisted. And she was right. So over the course of the next several months, April and I worked together to make changes in the law. I call that democracy in action: participatory, representative democracy—the system that has worked effectively in our country for more than 200 years.

Sometimes, constituents would call our office as a last resort. These calls often were out of desperation—citizens calling their state representative with nowhere else to turn. And often, we were able to help. One call was from a man who was literally on the verge of losing his home. The house had been sold at auction unbeknownst to him, and the bank, which now owned it, was about to move his furniture out on the lawn, totally confiscate the house, and leave his family homeless. He put out an S.O.S. to every legislator he could find; I was the only one who responded. The man actually had found an alternative way to pay for his home, but the foreclosure company wouldn't listen to him. They wouldn't listen to me at first, either.

"He doesn't have the money," the foreclosure bank assured me. "They never do. His house is ours now."

After a few tense weeks and many phone calls on behalf of this man and his family, I finally reached and spoke to someone from the foreclosure organization. They listened to my explanation and agreed to allow him to re-finance with his new ability to make the payments and stay in his home. As far as I know, he and his family live there to this day.

Several times, we came into contact with employees who had been mistreated by employers—good, solid workers being treated unfairly and fired on ridiculous, trumped-up charges. After collecting unemployment checks for several weeks, they had received the following information:

"You were fired because of misconduct. You will no longer receive unemployment checks and must now repay what you have already received."

This happened to several of my constituents, each one a single woman. These women had no idea how they would pay their current bills, let alone pay back the money already received and spent. They came to me in a state of hopelessness, dazed by the mistreatment they had suffered. I could read it in their eyes. One such woman would never have thought to call her state representative. I found out about it when I knocked on her door to ask if she needed help with anything.

My chief of staff, Chris Kilgroe, did extensive research on behalf of these workers and together we found a way to assist them. I even went to a hearing for one of the cases to observe how it was handled. There I learned that the woman who had done the firing had trumped up some bogus charges about the employee stealing paper plates, which the Administrative Law Judge could see right through. In this case, the woman was absolved, her unemployment checks were reinstated, and she could concentrate on finding new employment. The other cases were resolved in a similar manner. Each of these women is now employed in a new job. All any of them ever wanted was to work hard and be treated fairly.

I wonder what happens to similarly mistreated folks when a Republican holds this seat. Do they still have an ally in Lansing? All I know is that celebrating with these women after we had helped them get their lives back on track was a rich and satisfying experience—well worth the ordeal of being called every name in the books by my opponents and political enemies.

Another woman called our office (as a last resort) about her mother-in-law, who lived in Roosevelt Park, was a wonderful, well-loved woman with few resources and a house falling down around her. When the daughter-in-law called our office, my staff person at the time, Melissa Weipert, put in dozens of calls looking for ways to help this woman. I really have to hand it to Melissa. She so easily could have thrown in the towel on this stickler of a problem. But she kept making phone calls. In time, she contacted someone from Exit Realty and learned the company was looking for a house to make over, like the TV program does, as a way to advertise. Melissa put the agency in touch with the struggling woman and then Exit Realty went to work.

The result was fantastic. People donated materials, volunteers came in to help paint and repair, and before long this home had been given a complete makeover, with a new paint job, repairs to the home, and new appliances. They even added a little front porch. And just like in the TV show, a big truck was parked in front of her home, with friends and neighbors waiting on the other side of the truck to see her reaction. We yelled in unison: "Move that truck!" It pulled forward to reveal a like-new house for this deserving woman. She was thrilled beyond measure and simply couldn't stop smiling—both that day and whenever I run into her. Talk about job satisfaction! I was thrilled and proud that our office could be part of that transformation.

During my second term, when I was the chair of the Family and Children Services Committee, one constituent became a thorn in our sides—a man who had opened his home to his granddaughter and her baby, only to have the woman move out and take her now four-year-old son with her. She wouldn't allow her grandfather, who had been like a parent to that little boy, contact with her son. Of course, the man was bereft and heartbroken. He called often, begging us to enact some legislation that would provide him with the right to see his great-grandson. My staffer, Anne Pawli, a trained psychologist, spent many hours dealing with him, and we all felt sorry for his situation. But in the end, after hours of research and studying laws past and present, we had to admit there was little we could do for this man legislatively. Still, Anne faithfully talked to him on the phone for hours, essentially providing him with free therapy as he struggled with his grief.

Another woman called my office in tears. She was so upset she could barely talk. I had knocked on her door the previous year, and she remembered me and was calling for my help concerning a sticky child-custody issue related to a former spouse. I, of course, cannot determine anyone's custody, but by putting her in touch with the right people, she could resolve it herself. She just needed a little extra help to get going in the right direction—I was able to help her resolve this heart-searing issue with a few calls. The last time I talked with her, she was fine—and greatly relieved to have the issue behind her.

Needless to say, we weren't able to resolve every issue that came through the office. For the most part, people deeply appreciated our attempts to help. Some real bonds of friendship resulted. But sometimes, the person on the other end of the phone was furious with me and promised to ruin my reputation by reporting to all their friends and neighbors how horrid I was. No amount of apologizing or making a genuine effort to help could get them to change their minds about me. I had to learn an important lesson—for me at least—that I simply couldn't let those angry conversations get me down. I had to take the occasional diatribe. It helped that I was so busy—there was always so much work to be done that I couldn't dwell on unpleasant exchanges and incidents.

One issue, and the controversy it stirred up, created moments of conflict that still hurt me to this day. This was the issue of water rights—crucial to farmers, fishermen, boaters, and lakeshore residents—none of whom saw the issue from the same perspective.

Chapter XIV

Drink Up

I am back in downtown Lansing in the spring of 2011. The chicken salad sandwich I'm eating at the Grand Traverse Pie Company is filling my empty stomach and recharging my energy. It's a protest day. I'm here protesting another Republican assault on education—now they want to dramatically cut funding. After ten years of cuts, this will be the final nail in the coffin of many of our school districts.[15]

I'm also waiting for Cyndi Roper, Executive Director of Clean Water Action,[16] who agreed to join me for lunch. Cyndi was one of the first Lansing people I met when I ran for office the first time.

Shortly after I was elected, Cyndi came up to my office to fill me in on the latest threats regarding water diversion from the Great Lakes, one of the issues I had run on. Cyndi was—and still is—a joy to work with, deeply knowledgeable about water resources, without any sense of superiority about her

---

[15] My assessment about this was correct. Following this dramatic cut to funding, many schools were sent into deficit spending, and ultimately were taken over by the state via small-time dictators called Emergency Managers.

[16] Cyndi has since left Clean Water Action and is presently the Director for Michigan Voice.

expertise. Down to earth and strong in her beliefs about conservation, she remains completely amenable to reasonable compromise. We worked together to protect Michigan's water, celebrating the successes and commiserating after the defeats. She is committed to our waterways, and we are lucky to have her in Michigan. Now that I'm no longer a legislator, I put Cyndi in the friend column.

But today, we're talking about a new water battle concerning horizontal hydraulic fracking, a method used to squeeze every last bit of natural gas out of the earth. Both Cyndi and I believe that fracking in Michigan threatens to ruin our water quality. In horizontal hydraulic fracturing, or hydrofracturing (commonly called fracking), water is mixed with sand and chemicals, after which the mixture is injected at high pressure into a wellbore to create small fractures (typically less than 1mm), along which fluids such as gas, petroleum, and brine water migrate to be captured for our use. (This definition is from ask.com.) There is increasing evidence that fracking causes earthquakes—not to mention what can happen when broken pipes cause those chemicals to seep into the earth. When I was a state representative, that issue hadn't yet begun to rear its ugly head, so we focused more on how to strike a balance to keep industry strong while assuring Michigan's waters stay in Michigan.

The difficulty is that we can't limit water withdrawals without regulations. And without any limitations, outside companies can come into our state and take our water, drying up our lakes and rivers. Michigan Farm Bureau and Michigan Manufacturing, two powerful lobbying groups, seem to be against all regulation, all the time. Clearly, this creates a no-win impasse. Needless to say, the rich and powerful lobbying groups hold much more sway with legislators than poor environmental groups trying to make do with contributions from concerned citizens.

* * * *

Not long after taking office, I realized that water conservation was, and still is, one of the most contentious, emotional, and confusing issues facing our state. Michigan's water resources are part of our statewide identity—our history, our heritage, and our future. Water conservation issues strike at the very heart of who we are as Michiganians—the fishing, boating, agriculture, beer, paint, soft drink, and tourist industries all have a stake in this issue. They know that it's both the secret of our success as a state and key to continued prosperity.

A bit of history: when Europeans first settled in Michigan, they discovered a feast of natural resources for the taking, including shore-to-shore trees and beavers galore. Our ancestors depleted these resources and the industries they supported because they lacked foresight. The logging industry, in particular, chopped down whole forests with abandon and without a plan for replenishing them. It almost seemed like the rule of the day was: Whoever produces the most lumber makes the most money. As a result, forests were depleted and eventually, the lumber industry largely died out. The same can be said for beavers, which were trapped into near extinction for their pelts. Had we been smarter, we could have chopped down trees in a planned, organized fashion that would have better ensured the future of our natural forests. And still, the lumber barons could have become millionaires.

Now here we sit, in a brand new millennium, in a state surrounded by water: life-giving, beautiful, clean, sparkling, necessary water. Now is the time to decide whether we want to squander it or come up with a common-sense plan to preserve it for future generations. I fall clearly on the side of a common-sense approach to preserve it. I think most people agree with me.

But the companies that want to come here and pump millions of gallons of ground water out of Michigan don't want us to plan for our future; they want to be the millionaire lumber barons of the new millennium, at the expense of the people of Michigan. They consider legislators like me a real problem and think we should be voted out of office.

Today, we increasingly hear about the coming world water shortage. In the not-too-distant future, people near and far will want our water, and they'll want it in huge quantities. The contradiction between our need to use it and our need to protect it creates ongoing discord in Michigan. Awareness of this conflict came into focus in 1998 when (according to NPR's David Schaper in a July 8, 2008, news article) a Lake Superior-based company in Ontario proposed to take water by tanker out of Lake Superior to Asia.

Fortunately, the brakes were put on that project and Lake Superior was left alone. But the incident woke people up to the worldwide interest in our water resources, and the impact this could have on the Great Lakes. Many people also realized that no single state or country independently is able to stop the theft of water from the Great Lakes. So governing bodies from states and provinces that border one or more of the Great Lakes, as well as the Saint Lawrence River Basin, came together in December 2005 to draft an agreement: the "Great Lakes-St. Lawrence River Basin Sustainable Water Resources Agreement." The agreement banned water diversion out of the Great Lakes in containers greater than 5.7 gallons. But whether water in smaller bottles could be shipped out of the basin was left up to individual states. It is this arrangement that is commonly referred to as the "bottled water loophole."

To move the agreement forward and lay the groundwork for its success in Michigan, we needed to introduce relevant legislation. So in the summer of 2007 we held "rollouts": a series of press conferences across the entire state, one of which was held at Pere Marquette Park in Muskegon on a hot and windy July afternoon. Grand Rapids Representative Bob

Whenever a new piece of legislation came up, we had "roll-outs" across the state. Here is the roll-out for the water legislation. From the left, Speaker Pro Tem Mike Sak, me, Representative Bob Dean, Cyndi Roper from Clean Water Action.

Dean, Speaker Pro Tem Mike Sak, and I stood in the blowing sand, clutching our talking points against the sharp wind.

The *Chronicle* wasn't there, of course, but a Grand Rapids TV station showed up to cover the press conference. Mike

Sak began with a statement: "We are here today to talk about the precious water of our beautiful Great Lakes state. Many years ago, I promised myself I would do everything I could to protect Michigan's water. We are here today to discuss legislation to do just that."

He then briefly explained the purpose of the legislation, before introducing me.

"Thousands of gallons of water are taken out of the Great Lakes Basin every day, creating great risks for out trout streams, our water wells, and our own water supply," I began. I added facts and a few anecdotes to stress the urgency of this legislation. Then it was my turn to introduce State Representative Robert Dean.

He seconded what Mike and I had said and then Bob wrapped things up, after which we took questions from the conference attendees. We made similar appearances throughout the state, "rolling out" the bills so that folks would understand the importance of this legislation for Michigan's future.

A few days after we held our last press conference, the bills were "dropped" (legislative lingo meaning the bills were introduced). The day the bills came up in committee at the capitol, the meeting room was jam-packed with farmers, manufacturers, and well drillers, who were beyond distraught about the content of the legislation. Environmental advocates and those who loved fishing were there, too, along with others from the tourist industry, such as those with canoe and kayak rentals whose livelihoods depend on rivers and lakes maintaining their water flow. They wore smiles on their faces about making progress to keep our waterways safe from out-of-state interests who want our water and to keep their businesses strong.

Because of the sharp differences between the two groups, the bills were referred to a group formed to establish necessary compromises, a common practice in the legislature at that time. "Work groups" like this make the process of creating legislation lengthier, but in the end produce better legislation, because differing viewpoints are represented. In this case, Democratic Representative Rebekah Warren, then Chair of the House Great Lakes and Environment Committee, and Republican Senator Patti Birkholz, who was at that time Chair of the Senate Natural Resources, Environment and Great Lakes, worked on this legislation for months before it came back up in committee.

Initially, I thought the work group would be that small group around a table, putting their heads together to bring in good ideas and forge compromises. Due to the open meetings act, though, there is nothing small about a work group. Every lobbyist, staffer, and legislator—and their brothers and sisters, too—are at these formal work groups.

One of the hallmarks of this legislation was a one-of-a-kind computer tool (the brainchild of Senator Patti Birkholz) that could easily determine where groundwater was in short supply throughout the state. The computer pinpointed areas flush with water that wouldn't need extra regulation, as well as those areas that would require more cooperation in water use.

With this information, the two women established areas of agreement on all sides. Then they focused on differences of opinion, eventually finding ways to compromise that were acceptable. The two committee chairs brought the bills back to committee, where they passed, but the vote was far from unanimous. In fact, all the Republican representatives voted against it, in addition to the Democratic Jackson Representative Marty Griffin. Through this tough process, an odd group of unlikely allies finally got the legislation passed: environmentalists, trout fishers, and concerned citizens.

Enacting the water compact would have been a perfect opportunity for Michigan to put further protections into place, such as a provision to put Michigan's groundwater in the public trust. Sadly, the water barons won that battle; the legislation didn't put our groundwater in the public trust, despite the fact that surface water rights have been in the public trust for decades. Have surface water rights interfered with the rights of landowners? Of course not. Has it deprived us of any rights at all? No. Has it restricted our freedoms? No. What it has done is ensure that our Michigan water stays in Michigan. It also gives citizens the right to keep the surface water clean.

We currently need to do the same with the water under the earth—groundwater—to prevent lakes, rivers, and streams from being depleted.

Vermont has had legislation to protect their groundwater for several years. It has neither destroyed the state economy nor caused anyone to tax it. Most important, it has kept Vermont's water in Vermont, where it belongs. My sister, Jeanne Rindell, a Vermont resident, recently expressed to me her deep appreciation of this protection to their water. This sort of legislation is precisely what Michigan needs. But those who want to make a profit from our water have used the reliable and effective tactic of fear mongering to keep our water available for *their* taking.

During the process of passing this legislation, I lost a good deal of respect for Michigan's Farm Bureau. As I said earlier, individual farmers are some of the most hard-working, salt-of-the-earth people I ever dealt with in office; I came to admire and respect them. The Farm Bureau as an organization, though, in my opinion, was less than honest with the farmers as it relates to this issue.

Here is an example: While the legislation was still being worked on, several Michigan farmers called to tell me that the legislation would be disastrous for them because during the summer months they needed to use more water than the bill allowed, which would cause their crops to die. "That would be a disaster," I agreed.

I quickly set about changing the legislation to better protect agricultural interests in my district. I learned the legislation already contained a waiver for farmers during the summer months. When the callers learned the truth, they were satisfied.

No sooner did that controversy die down, than another call came in from a scared and desperate farmer. "I heard that if my water pump breaks I will have to get a permit to replace it, which could take days or even weeks. I use water every single day and cannot afford to be without it while I am waiting for a permit."

Once again, I looked into the legislation to see if his concern was founded. It was not. "That part of the bill has already been fixed," Committee Chair Rebekah Warren told me. Sure enough, the little glitch in that particular bill had been repaired. No one would have to seek a permit when the pump broke. I told the farmer not to worry about permits for water pumps, but I could tell that his distrust of the government was so deep that he didn't fully believe me.

Calls like this went on for weeks. I finally came to the conclusion that Farm Bureau lobbyists must have been stirring people up with false information. In vain, I tried to sit down with the Farm Bureau lobbyist myself to see if we could come up with some sort of a compromise on the issue of water regulation.

"No compromises," I was told. "We are against all regulation all the time, no matter the reason." Slam. The door was shut. I asked if this was true even when water-thirsty potato farms are competing for water with fragile trout streams. I brought this up as an example of a situation when some sort of compromise might be essential. Trout streams are fragile. If the water level drops, trout die. Potato farmers use an enormous amount of water. So wherever potatoes farmers are near trout streams, discussion is in order. The Farm Bureau was adamant. No compromise.

The Farm Bureau wields enormous power in the state. They own enough legislators in Lansing from both parties to stall any legislation that requires regulation related to agriculture. Individual farmers might have been more amenable to this legislation if they had had a sharper understanding of the issue and been given honest information.

Most farmers do everything necessary to preserve Michigan's clean water supply. They understand the importance of preserving resources. But the essential dilemma facing our state is this: Unfortunately, some farmers don't care about the environment and thus their farming methods may create massive pollution problems. Because the good farmers want no regulation, the bad farmers get away with water pollution. In addition, water withdrawal for profit could create unchecked disasters.

We all want our water to remain in Michigan. We also want our state industries and agricultural endeavors to thrive. It shouldn't have been so difficult to strike a compromise—a deal in which farmers can work their land and prosper, and our water remains here for the citizens of the Great Lakes region. The Farm Bureau blocked, and continues to block, such a compromise.

Despite the Farm Bureau's lobbying and fear mongering, Governor Granholm signed the package of bills to preserve Michigan's water into law. Again, some felt the legislation was weak and unsatisfactory, but it was the best we could do with the all-powerful Farm Bureau blocking progress at every turn. A public signing event was held in Saugatuck on the shores of Lake Michigan. The cool breeze tempered the hot sun and ruffled the paperwork of the bills as Governor Jennifer Granholm signed the package of bills into law.

In fact, eventually the entire compact was signed into law on October 3, 2008, by then-president George W. Bush. When I think of how difficult it can be to get legislation through two chambers and a governor, I have to admit it took a small miracle to get agreement on water regulation legislation from eight states, two provinces, and two countries.

Several years ago, Nestle Waters North America came into Michigan's Mecosta County and began pumping water out of the ground. They drew out thousands of gallons, bottled it up under the name "Ice Mountain," and put it on the market. Invasive actions such as this run the risk of harming the ecosystem and reducing water levels. They can narrow streams, expose mud flats, and reduce flow levels. The reason the company could come into the area was that Michigan had so few water protections in place for groundwater extraction. That is what we tried to correct, and only partially corrected, by passing water legislation.

The issue remained thorny through my second term. And, though I had the wisdom to spare myself grief by not co-sponsoring Brenda Clack's homeschooling legislation during my first term, I eagerly signed Representative Dan Scripps' legislation to put water in the public trust during my second term. I am fully in favor of keeping our beer, paint, agriculture, and pop economies strong and vibrant, even though these products send water out of Michigan. I am staunchly on the side of assuring our farmers earn money from their land and the manufacturing industry thrives. At the same time, I want to ensure that big corporations from other countries cannot come here and steal our water. I think that's what we all want—a balanced approach to the problem.

Currently water diversions are small and aren't emptying our Great Lakes. Water-bottling companies claim that shipping water out of state will never become a problem due to the high cost of shipping. The truth, though, is that as water becomes scarcer, demand, of course, will grow—which is likely to drive up the price and make shipping it out of the state worth the expense. We know that water withdrawals can destroy small lakes, rivers, and streams. Wells can go dry and neighboring farms be put at risk of water shortage. Why not put common-sense measures in place right now?

Those who are driven by the profit motive to take our water don't want citizens to understand the issue. So they create bogus and ridiculous fears about putting water in the public trust. The most absurd assertion is that ground water will become something that is taxed. This is ridiculous beyond all measure. As far as I know, nobody in Michigan wants ground water taxed—it has never been whispered, talked about, hinted at, or even thought of. The idea that putting ground water in the public trust will lead to taxing it is ridiculous. But those who would take our water away from us have used it as an effective fear tactic. Unfortunately, many voters accepted the water tax lie as truth. We heard it repeatedly during my campaign for state senate.

"Why does Mary Valentine want to tax our water?" they'd ask.

"Mary Valentine would never tax your water," was the correct answer.

Sadly, Dan Scripps' water conservation legislation, which I co-sponsored, died in committee. Goeff Hansen, my political opponent during the race for state senate, and the Republican Party knew that the legislation had failed to come out of committee, but they decided to play on voters' fears about taxing water to win votes.

We, as Michigan citizens, are still vulnerable; our water is free for the taking. We need to educate ourselves on these issues if we want our children and grandchildren to swim, kayak, sail, and walk along the beaches of our precious shorelines and riverbanks. If we want them to skip stones, have a campfire by the lake, and take pictures of the sun setting into the water, as my children have done, we'll need to stand strong together.

Chapter XV

The "T" Word

I've watched Michigan's 46th Legislature, which immediately followed my time in office, move us quickly toward shrinking our middle class and expanding the poverty class.

It's November 2011. Just yesterday I found myself at the Capitol Building once again—this time to attend a hearing on a bill that will further gut workers' compensation. The stories people bring to the capitol tear my heart out. A police officer shot at and beaten in his effort to serve and protect has been on workers' comp several times. As soon as he was able, he went back to work. The compensation he received until he was ready to work again kept his family financially viable while he recovered. This is an example of what the new legislature wants to end.

An older woman who had worked all her life until she was injured on the job also testified. At first, no one had questioned her injury or her inability to work; they had allowed her to receive a disability payment of around $200 per week. Then the rules had started changing. She had received less and less compensation for her on-the-job injury—until finally, her compensation had shrunk to, I sadly recall, in the neighborhood of $4.95 a month. I wonder if Senators Phil Pavlov and Goeff Hansen could support themselves on $4.95 a month. That's what they codified into law.

This is the new "pro-family" legislation Republican leadership has brought to Michigan working families. Today, I am recovering from the disheartening realities I witnessed in Lansing yesterday. And I am beyond heartbroken.

But something else happened. After the hearing, I went to the balcony overlooking the House chamber to seek consolation. I looked up at the gorgeous stained glass ceiling, with the name and symbol of each state etched upon it to inspire current and future leaders. I tried to feel a sense of hope, even though I believe our hard-won democracy is now going in the wrong direction, with "pro-family" legislators ripping away at the needs of working families. Our embattled middle class is shrinking by the hour. I want to be hopeful. I want to feel like our democracy is still intact. I know that if people work hard together, they can still put Michigan back on a path that will truly help our families, not just use their struggle as a talking point at election time.

The majesty of the Capitol Building restored my sense of hope for our future.

* * * *

One of the first things I learned when I took office in 2007 was the hard truth that Michigan was in a terrible financial mess. We were at the bottom of a 24-year-old downward spiral, leaving behind the forward-looking Michigan of Soapy Williams, James Blanchard, and William Milliken. I was unknowingly walking into a financial disaster.[17]

It wasn't always so. In fact, in the early 1980s, Michigan was a beacon of prosperity to the states surrounding us.

---

[17] As I write this, four years later, our financial mess still concerns me. We were underfunded in 2007; we are even more underfunded now.

People had jobs, our state coffers were full, and the state government had a plethora of good workers. It wasn't wise, in light of that financially healthy scenario, to pass another tax increase, but that is what the Democrats did at that time. Soon Michigan citizens (with the help, it is rumored, of then-Senator John Engler) sprang into action against these new taxes. Recalls were enacted, and in the end, two Democratic senators were recalled and replaced by Republicans. The Senate flipped to Republican control, where it has remained ever since. When the Republicans first took charge, Michigan was a progressive state on solid ground. We had good roads, top-notch education, consumer protections, and a strong heritage of clean air and water. Our public health department added years to peoples' lives and our strong community mental health programs helped people receive critical services, keeping them alive and their families strong.

Since the 1980s however, we have been in continual decline. In the past few decades, the drama surrounding Michigan taxes has been intense. Those recalls in the 1980s have caused the very word "tax" to strike fear into the heart of every legislator—which is why the word is rarely used in any campaign, or even policy discussion. Instead, politicians call tax increases "revenue enhancements," a euphemism straight from the Republican playbook. Because of the memory of those ugly recalls, Michigan's mantra has been "no new taxes" (or revenue enhancements). Ever. Instead, the idea is to cut services harshly, then cut, and cut again. A few early cuts weren't terribly damaging, but now we are losing crucial services and protections. As citizens of this great state, we need to decide what's important for our families and children. I understand well that in some situations taxes become too burdensome and can stifle the economy. But if we take that thinking to the extreme, the result is no services, fewer jobs, and no progress. And that, in my opinion, is what we are looking at in Michigan today.

The endless cuts to revenue and services had already put us in a perilous state when the auto industry, our bread and butter for more than 100 years, collapsed, which resulted in a further loss of state revenue. Michigan could solve this problem with a small, temporary tax increase. The days of using common sense to solve thorny problems, however, are gone. In the current legislature, ideology trumps common sense every time. So the crisis continues. Services continue to shrink and cuts to public schools, public health, public roads, public safety, and well, public everything—have become severe. We robbed from Peter to pay Paul, emptied every rainy-day fund we could find, and exhausted all of our resources. And still, the Republicans wanted to cut taxes and services.

When I came into office, local leaders from all levels of government begged me not to make additional cuts. Township, city, and county governments, the public health department, schools at every level from preschool through community colleges and universities, fire departments, police departments, libraries, cooperative extension, and senior resources—the leaders of every one of those programs were calling my office and begging me not to make further cuts to services and programs.

"There is nothing left to cut, Mary," each of them said in their own way. "We are down to the bone."

Every knowledgeable person knew that state revenues, between income tax cuts and the fall of the auto industry, had been cut in half. Still, Republicans continued to spread the lie that Jennifer Granholm had expanded the state budget.

Michigan is one of the few states with a flat income tax.

At one time it had been over 6%. When I came into office, it was down to 3.9%, one of the lowest flat income tax rates in the country, which had caused a $1.8 billion hole in the budget. If the Democrats had gone too far in raising taxes in the early 1980s, the Republicans were clearly now going too far in the opposite direction. It irked me that Republican politicians perpetuated the myth that spending had *increased* under Governor Jennifer Granholm. The truth was that state spending had decreased by half since the early 2000s. The money coming into the state from the federal government had increased, which is what the Republicans were referring to, successfully misleading the voters.

Logic demands an admission that as a state we have gone too far and we must find a way to restore lost revenue. It's the same approach I'd use if I couldn't make my house payment. First I would cut my spending, as the state has already done, then I'd find things to sell off or figure out how to create more income. Or both. But I would do *something*. I wouldn't stick my head in the sand and hope for a miracle. Neither would you.

But that is essentially what the Republicans did by refusing to even consider the option of additional taxes.

"Run government like a business," they say.

I have news for them. Government is not a business; it is a service. Government doesn't exist for the purpose of making a profit, as business does. The only way for government to bring money in is to levy taxes or increase fees. We could sell off our state parks or our public roads, or maybe the Mackinaw Bridge. I don't want to do that and I don't think you do, either.

We are left with an age-old solution: The people of Michigan pitch in to get us through this challenging time in our economy.

Too many Republicans, with their majority in the Senate, were adamant about over-spending, convinced that all we had to do was find more ways to cut—no matter how many good services went down the drain, no matter how much our citizens suffered, no matter whose wages got reduced. This was bad enough, but by early 2007, we also had former state legislator and tax nut, Leon Drolet, to contend with while the controversy raged about the $1.8 billion hole in the budget. He had a 20-foot-high pink plastic pig named "Porky" that he dragged to our districts with the incessant cry of "recall" on his lips. He personally threatened to organize a recall on every legislator who voted for a tax increase.

Democrats, of course, were terrified of recalls—terrified of losing our majority in the House and the opportunity to pass much-needed progressive legislation to move the state forward. The recalls of the early 1980s were at the heart of our fear. All our hopes and dreams were down the drain if some of us got recalled and we lost our majority in the middle of the term. As a new state representative, I was constantly coached on how to talk about this. Never, ever, under any circumstances, I was told, should I talk publicly about raising taxes. Don't even say the word aloud. This was drummed into my head day and night.

The drama built by the month. Make more cuts or bring in the necessary revenues to run the state and face a recall. About this time bumper stickers starting appearing on cars owned by Republican legislators: *Friends Don't Let Friends Raise Taxes.* Tax policy is complex and consequential; yet, some Republican legislators preferred to sum up the entire challenge with a six-word phrase. *Friends Don't Let Friends Raise Taxes.* This was about as helpful as a pink pig named Porky.

I always assumed that restoring a small part of the income tax that had been cut during the previous legislature would be a reasonable solution to our current financial crisis, along with some additional cuts and reforms to systems that were too expensive. But I quickly learned how deep passions ran about an income tax increase. The Chamber of Commerce, along with Republican legislators, seemed convinced that Michigan would be destroyed if we raised taxes even a smidgeon. Others threw their hands up in despair and expressed deep hatred for all politicians.

The County Road Association of Michigan (CRAM) began sending symbols of our crumbling infrastructure to our offices. Every week a new symbol showed up in my mailbox: one week it would be a miniature trash barrel, the next a piece of crumbling road. Once they even sent a miniature toilet. For months on end they came, reminding us of the dire state of Michigan's infrastructure and the need to find funds to rebuild our roads, dams, and bridges.

Of course, we also received pleas from teachers and parents; they poured in by snail mail, e-mail, and phone. Please, no more cuts to our schools. The Department of Human Services (DHS) board also contacted me regularly, begging me not to further cut services to Michigan's needy residents. Senior Resources explained and re-explained all the ways that senior citizens would suffer if their resources were cut again. Every Town Hall I attended, every coffee hour, I heard repeatedly that further cuts wouldn't be endurable. Every organization that came to Lansing presented us with graphs and statistics showing us why *their* program should be preserved above all others. In fact, the most bothersome discussions were with those who insisted we cut everyone else's revenues—just not theirs. If they alone were spared from sweeping cuts, all would be well. All the others were just wasting taxpayer money, of course.

So I hosted a Town Hall meeting in which all parties asking not to be cut presented their cases to the public. I think I successfully put out the message that this was a challenge facing *all* of us, not just one group or another.

And all the while, Leon Drolet kept dragging his pink pig around the state, threatening recalls of anyone who voted to restore revenues. It would have made common sense for us to get the budget set by July 1st. That deadline came and went. No resolution. The impasse dragged on, the drama continued, month after precious month.

I weighed every idea that came in, listened to all suggestions, and heard heartbreaking stories of decimated families. I continued to believe that along with some reasonable cuts and reforms, restoring a slightly higher income tax, as Michigan's legislature had done in the past, would be a relatively painless way to get our state beyond the impasse.

A few constituents asked me to raise taxes for the sake of the state, and a few asked me not to, but both groups were a minority. The vast majority of people were somewhere in the middle and supported a combination of these three things: reductions (further cuts), reform (change methods that were overly expensive), and revenues (a politically correct word for taxes). So that's the position I supported.

My caucus panicked. "If you vote for taxes you *will* get recalled, Mary," they insisted. "You simply cannot withstand a recall election. If, by some strange twist of fate, you don't get recalled, you'll never be able to get re-elected, which means all our shared hopes and dreams to correct drug company immunity, stop out-of-state-trash from coming into our state, and fund necessary programs would be dashed. Please don't ever vote for tax increases. We need you here in Lansing."

It was tough for me. Truthfully, it was tough for all of us.

But it was excruciating for those of us from "marginal" seats. These are the seats that tend to swing from Democrat to Republican, which we could easily lose if we weren't careful, ending our ability to set any agenda. The eight "marginals" in the House during my first term were under intense scrutiny—from our supporters, our constituents, and our caucus, all pulling us in different directions.

The thinking among the Democratic leadership at the time was that if we could find six Republicans with a conscience to vote for new taxes, we marginals wouldn't have to go up as green on the voting board. So Andy Dillon pushed—for months—to get a few Republicans to vote yes. I can see now that this was a foolish strategy. Maybe our leader privately wanted to hurt the Democrats so that the Republicans would win big in the next election. I don't know. But if that was his strategy, it was effective—the Republicans won everything in the 2010 election. Andy Dillon, incidentally, became State Treasurer for a time.

The absolutely drop-dead budget deadline is always October 1, after which the state government no longer has money to operate and shuts down. The situation in Lansing didn't get better as that deadline loomed. Raise revenues, cut vital services, the pink pig, and *Friends Don't Let Friends Raise Taxes*. At times, it felt like being on an out-of-control merry-go-round.

As August turned into September and we still had no resolution, our leadership kept us in the capitol around the clock. They put air mattresses in the Speaker's Library and brought in pizzas and pop. Strategy after strategy failed as we attempted to get a few more Republican votes.

Once, leadership even tried a "call of the house." This is when all legislators are locked in the chamber, and whoever isn't present must return to the chamber. If the legislators cannot be found, state police are sent to bring them back to the capitol, at which time the doors are shut, locking them in. State Representative Rebekah Warren was called back from her honeymoon in Europe, but State Representative Dave Aegema, on a sheep-hunting expedition in Russia, couldn't be found.

One strategy our leadership wanted us to try got me into hot water with my supporters at home. At this point, I had been in Lansing eight whole months and trusted the more experienced among us. You know, the ones who had been here four years already.[18]

In caucus, we decided that when the revenue bill came up, the marginals would stay off the voting board, which supposedly would force some Republicans to vote yes. Apparently, the thinking of those in charge was that some Republican would step up and vote for revenues if the marginals refrained from voting. *Then,* we were told, the budget would be decided on time. A vote was called and others voted, but we, the marginals, didn't vote; we stayed off the board for three full days. Somehow, we thought this would force some well-meaning Republicans to vote yes, so the revenue bill would pass and the state wouldn't shut down. During these three days, the media went crazy.

This provided a great opening for the Republican-friendly political reporter from the *Chronicle*, who would move mountains to make me look bad. He described what was happening (on the front page of the paper) by inferring that I didn't care enough about my district to even vote. Oh, joy! Here I

---

[18] In Michigan, state representatives are term-limited after three terms, so at the beginning of a new term, these with four years of experience are the old pros. That's ridiculous, of course, for something as complex as legislating the laws of the state.

was up around the clock, camped out at the state capitol, keeping constituents informed about what was really happening, rather than the fiction being promoted by the Republicans. And the news is that I don't care enough to vote?

At this point, my supporters joined the news media in going crazy. *What are you doing? Why won't you vote for taxes? Have you changed since you've been down there? Where's the Mary we donated money to and knocked doors for?* I made a personal call to every single person who contacted me to explain the situation's complexities. I generally started with the same line: "The reporter from the *Chronicle* doesn't want me to get re-elected. That's why he wrote the story that way."

Calls poured into the office from all directions. I returned calls from my office phone, my mobile phone, and my home phone. Call, call, call. Try to straighten this out. An e-mail or written response of any kind simply wasn't good enough.

Meanwhile, with "Porky" permanently stationed in front of the capitol, the merry-go-round kept spinning. The bumper sticker *Friends Don't Let Friends Vote for Taxes* adorned more cars. News trucks from around the state lined the streets around the capitol. Superintendents, teachers, and principals called me: *Please, Mary, no further cuts.* Public safety personnel called me: *If you cut us, you put our families at risk.*

The infrastructure items continued to pour into our mailboxes.

We struggled through September. About midway through September, we got word that this was it. We would, on that very day, be holding the vote about taxes. The caucus was adamant in their belief that I couldn't survive a recall and that it would cost them hundreds of thousands of dollars trying to defend my seat if I voted yes on any new taxes.

I felt like I was going off to war that day. Everyone I ran

into shook my hand and said, "I know you will make the right decision, Mary."

I heard it before I left my office and again on the elevator. I heard it again as I crossed the street to the capitol and several more times before I actually entered it. By the time I climbed the back stairs and arrived in the chamber, I was prepared for a battle. Once in the chamber, I noticed the galleries filled with lobbyists and spectators, each dedicated to a different agenda. My phone kept ringing and my inbox was flooded with e-mails from constituents begging for no further cuts.

But on that day, and several subsequent days, we didn't actually take the dreaded vote. Instead, our leaders bargained all night long while we slept on air mattresses in the Speaker's Library. Even our colleague Barb Byrum, who was now several months pregnant with her first child, slept on an air mattress. And we all worried about our friend and colleague Aldo Vagnossi, who, in his 80s, was struggling with liver cancer.

After several nights, at around 11:00 p.m., while we still sat at our desks, my organizer, Jen Patterson, came in grinning. Apparently, she had been talking to some of Leon Drolet's supporters who were hanging around the pink pig parked in front of the capital. Rumor had it that I would vote for tax increases that very night. Drolet's people were thrilled. As soon as that happened, she relayed, the recall would start, and they could earn money organizing for my recall election. I was thrilled, of course, to hear this tiny morsel of information about my future.

When it started to really sink in that I would likely face a recall if I voted for the tax increase, I was deeply upset. I had worked so hard to win this seat and tried so hard to bring a new, fresh voice to Lansing. I could see the headlines in the

Chronicle: "Mary Valentine Being Recalled." I worried that people would think I had done something so morally wrong that I deserved to be recalled. I had wanted to serve; I had wanted to make things better. It seemed so unfair given how committed I was to being a good representative for my district.

In time, I calmed down and came to my senses. I remembered that any human being might be called on at any moment to do the right thing and face negative consequences for it. If this was my moment, I was prepared.

Republicans in the Michigan legislature had been "starving the beast" for years, denying financial support to public coffers no matter what, until services were cut to their nub. I knew that I would vote as I believed and as my constituents wanted me to vote. Leon Drolet and his band of young, clean-cut, ill-informed followers wouldn't control me.

One of the late nights, at 4:00 a.m. to be exact (after many sleepless nights), we were in the caucus room, hashing this out. The caucus leaders, who had come to my district to knock doors, had helped me raise money, and had made my political life possible, still insisted I vote no on new tax revenues. In my best middle-of-the-night, sleepless way, I tried to explain why I needed to vote yes—and that I hoped for the support of the leadership when I voted. It was pretty simple: My constituents wanted and needed a yes vote, and they were whom I was working for. Because I wasn't a professional politician, it seemed clear to me. Vote for the well being of the people of my district. I knew I should be voting for them, re-election or not, recall or not.

Suddenly, my voice broke. Tears sprang out of my eyes and simply wouldn't stop. I sat right there in caucus and sobbed for a half-hour. I was way too tired to even care how it appeared to others. I just wanted the support of my colleagues for doing what I knew to be the right thing. My intensity on that night even earned me the nickname "conscience of the caucus" to some. Finally, halfway through the day on September 30—the last day to solve the budget dilemma before the government shut down—Representative Andy Meisner of Ferndale led a movement on the House floor.

"Let's pull the trigger," he said.

So we did. After all those months, we actually did something. We voted for tax increases. Two Republicans with a conscience joined the Democrats and voted yes. I voted with the caucus' blessing, and most of the other marginals did the same. The bills were sent to the Senate, where they also gained the support of enough Republicans to pass. Governor Granholm signed them into law.

Sigh of relief.

Taxes raised by a hair and vital services protected—for a while anyway. We had to adjust some of our decisions, but a complete shutdown of the government was avoided. A year later, the worldwide economy crashed and the same problems emerged on a national level. Interestingly, Republican legislators in Michigan blamed the worldwide economic collapse on that slight tax increase in our state. They never cease to amaze me.

And yes, the recall attempts came: Bob Dean, Mary Valentine, Marc Couriveau, Andy Dillon, Marie Donigan, anyone who voted for taxes, as promised. Recalls bounced around our caucus like a ping-pong ball gone wild. The antidote, as usual, was for us to talk to constituents at their doors. We walked our districts, went to our colleagues' districts and knocked doors for them, and used this as an opportunity to raise money. In the end, no one was recalled. My recall didn't even get approval (based on vague wording), which was a happy relief. Andy Dillon's recall made it to the ballot, but he beat it. The recall attempts were successful, though, in that they cost our caucus a lot of money in lawyer fees. And as I had been warned, my vote caught up with me. Not right away—I won my first re-election despite my vote on taxes—but the issue came back to haunt me big time in the Senate campaign.

But in the fall of 2007, with the tax vote finally behind us, the legislature got back to the work of legislating. Our economy had been overly reliant on the auto industry for too long; diversifying our economy was at the top of our must-do list. Moving toward renewable energy would clean up our air and water and bring jobs as well, a wonderful win-win opportunity for our great state. And the film industry was on its way to Michigan. It was a perfect fit.

A Final Note about the "T" Word

During a small, poorly attended, and unadvertised forum in downtown Muskegon, I had a terrible encounter with the "T" word. It was October 2008. After two years in office, I fell victim to something I had rarely experienced in all my years in the legislature—overconfidence. I stopped being careful about every single word that escaped my lips, and let my guard down.

My opponent, Holly Hughes, was there, as well as her supporters, videotaping every word I said. Those of us running for state representative in both the 91st and 92nd districts were there, discussing numerous topics, including taxes, but I thought it went well. When the forum ended I took my seat next to my daughter, Robin.

"Mom, did you know you just said that you voted for taxes as often as you could?" she asked.

That one misspoken word occurred during the '08 campaign, when Cecelia Fierro was our Emily's List Volunteer. She came to be like a member of our family. She's now studying for her law degree.

I could hardly believe her. Is that what I had said? But she was right.

How had I come to say such a thing? It wasn't true! In retrospect, I realized what happened. I had meant to say that I voted *against* tax increases as often as I could. A one-word mistake—but what a crucial word!

When I realized my error, I was devastated. After the forum, I went directly home and cried my heart out. I felt like I was the worst person in the world and had let down all the wonderful people who had contributed so generously to my campaign. All of the people who believed in me—I had completely let them down. Robin and Chris Kilgroe tried to console me and to tell me that everything would be okay. But I was inconsolable for the rest of that day.

In the end, of course, I picked myself up, dried my tears, dusted myself off, and continued my campaign work, knocking on doors to talk to voters and making calls to raise the money I needed to earn a second term.

Holly Hughes and her team used my error well. They created a TV ad with me saying that I had voted for taxes. They used it in a robo call and plastered it on their lit pieces. It was so embarrassing for me, being constantly reminded of my mistake. But at the end of the day, my hard work knocking on doors and being available to my constituents paid off. Despite the gaffe, I was reelected to a second term.

The real consequence for this slip-up came during my Senate campaign. My opponents used the statement repeatedly, and it took a toll. Would I have had a better chance of winning my Senate race if it had never happened? I'll never know.

Chapter XVI

Hollywood of the Midwest?

"Push 'em back. Push 'em back. Push 'em waaaaaaaaaay back."

My dad always repeated that cheer during the football games we watched together when I was kid. The fall after my dad died, my son, Shawn, played defense on the Mona Shores football team. Every time they were in one of those precarious defense positions, I'd hear my dad's words echo in my ears. "Push 'em back. Push 'em back. Push 'em waaaaay back." I missed him. But allowing memories to surface was part of the healing.

This is what it's like now, easing my way back into civilian life. I see, hear, or smell something that transports me back in time to the years I served in the legislature. The other day, I saw Mitch Albom on TV advocating for continuing the rebates that brought the film industry to Michigan. He had talked to the governor about it, but Governor Snyder had ignored Mitch and went on to crush Michigan's budding film industry by chopping the rebates. Within months of taking office, Republican leadership cut the juicy film rebates to tiny allotments that would no longer draw Hollywood moviemakers to Michigan. Anyone who knew anything about this knew that without large rebates, the film industry would leave Michigan—which it did.

Mary Valentine

The whole idea of bringing the film industry to Michigan in the first place was bipartisan, brought to us by Republican Bill Huizinga, now 2nd Congressional District Congressman, and Democrat Andy Meisner, now the Treasurer of Oakland County. They were both in their third and final terms as state representatives and they worked across the aisle to achieve this goal. I remember how it started as though it were yesterday.

* * * *

I hopped off the elevator and walked into Commerce Committee (Room 519 in the House Office Building) to see Mitch Albom, *Detroit Free Press* sports writer, and actor Jeff Daniels talking with the committee chair, Andy Meisner. They had come to Lansing to convince us that we needed to bring the film industry to Michigan and to teach us how to do it. I had loved Jeff Daniels' film *Escanaba in Da Moonlight,* with its familiar Upper Peninsula setting. Mitch Albom's bestseller, *Tuesdays With Morrie,* had gently walked me through the difficult experience of losing my beloved father. Needless to say, I was thrilled to have the opportunity to meet these two celebrities. And yes, I was intensely interested in what they had to say—but I was also star-struck.

Representative Meisner called the meeting to order and asked Mitch Albom to testify. First, Albom explained why he and Jeff Daniels had come together to promote the film industry in Michigan. "We both write screenplays and want to have them produced in Michigan. But producers will make their movies only in the states that offer the best tax rebates, and Michigan's rebates are puny and ineffective."

As a result, he explained, even though his movies were about Michigan, they were filmed elsewhere. Both men were convinced that the film industry was a good idea for Michigan's economy, with its need to diversify and create jobs. And Michigan has a great variety of settings—from the Great Lakes' shorelines, to downtown Detroit, to small towns and farms of the midland.

Our guests also told us that on the rare occasions movies had been made in Michigan, the producers had been astonished by the work ethic of their Michigan employees—folks who got to work on time, sought extra work, and gave their full measure every day. Hollywood was hungry for the Michigan work ethic. Last but not least, we had empty factories galore in our state, ready and waiting to be remade into film studios.

"When a film comes to a town," Albom told us, "it brings jobs, and lots of them: film jobs, such as filming, producing, sound, lighting, and acting; jobs for extras, gaffs, grips, electricians, and truckers; and ancillary jobs by the hundreds. Because the large cast and crew need to be fed, they'll need caterers. The hairdressing, construction, car rental, restaurant, and hotel industries all benefit when a movie production comes to town. All those people then make money, which they spend in the local community. The filmmakers can create production studios in old factories. Everyone wins."

"Also," Albom added, "it's a clean industry. It doesn't ruin our air and water or cause costly cleanups. And it can get here quickly—no factories to build, no train tracks to lay, no water and sewers to upgrade. We give the tax rebates. Filmmakers will come."

"Finally," he said, "films bring tourists." I remembered visiting the tiny town of Big Bay, on the shores of Lake Superior, where the Academy-Award-winning film *Anatomy of a Murder* was filmed more than 50 years ago. Since then, the town has become a tourist destination. Fifty years later, tourists still visit to see where Gregory Peck stayed during the movie's filming.

"But the tax incentives must be generous," Albom warned us that day, "or the movie industry simply won't come. Never mind that we have great settings, the best workers in the country, and empty factories waiting to be turned into film studios. Film companies will only come if we offer them substantial incentives. That's just the way it works."

Jeff Daniels put in his two cents worth. "You will know you've arrived when advertisements are made here and TV series come," he said. "These projects bring the jobs that are steady and lucrative."

"But the film industry is finicky," they warned us. "They can come on a dime; but they can pull up stakes in a heartbeat as well."

What was not to like about this idea? I was excited from the first moment I heard it. I also was aching to tell Mitch Albom what his book *Tuesdays with Morrie* had meant to me personally. Finally, at the end of the hour-and-a-half-long committee meeting, a burning question popped into my head. I no longer remember the question, but I remember what I said after the question.

"Mr. Albom, *Tuesdays with Morrie* was one of the best books I have ever read," I said. And I meant it.

He beamed.

Jeff Daniels and Mitch Albom came back one more time to testify before our committee. This time we went to the stately appropriations hearing room in the Capitol Building, which took on a circus-like atmosphere because of all the media and visitors who had come to see the stars.

In time, the bills passed through both chambers, nearly unanimously, and were signed into law by Governor

Granholm. I was thrilled to have my name on one of the bills, but then learned that the Senate had promised to block the legislation unless my name was taken off. I guess they were afraid this could boost my re-election campaign. The pettiness of this irked me, but I have to admit, I was flattered in a weird way that they were intimidated by little old me.

After we passed the bills, the film industry came to Michigan in droves. Our young people came back to Michigan. People got hired to be extras, gaffs, grips, producers, and camera workers. I heard about a woman who received $1,000 as an extra and had the delightful experience of working with Drew Barrymore for a day. Clint Eastwood came to Michigan to film *Gran Torino*. *Conviction*, starring Hillary Swank, was filmed in Grand Rapids.

And as Mr. Daniels had predicted, within two years, Detroit was the proud home of a series set in Detroit and made in Detroit, *Detroit 1-8-7*—a story about the trials and tribulations of Detroit's homicide unit. Michigan's film industry was off and running.

As everyone had hoped, the film incentives brought jobs, put Michigan on the map, and lifted our spirits as a state. Studios were built, which gave jobs to construction trade workers. Teamsters' jobs increased. Universities offered classes to give students the skills they needed to break into the industry. Homegrown talent was evident as young people got jobs on big films. It was exciting to watch the steady growth of the industry, an upward trajectory that quickly put Michigan on the map—and on the radar of film producers everywhere.

In the end, though, shallow talking points led to the demise of the film industry in Michigan. The goal of inviting the film industry to come here, from day one, was to create jobs. That's what it did. But some believed the goal behind the arrangement was to bring revenues into the state coffers. They railed against the expense of the film industry, claiming that Michigan was spending too much money for each job created. The truth is, it *was* expensive at first. In time, though, once established, those incentives could have been lowered. With the film industry firmly established here, more jobs would have come at less of a cost. And for years to come, it would have been a huge boost to our tourist trade. But some criticized the industry and strove to drive it out of Michigan. This was particularly true of Senator Nancy Cassis, Republican from Novi, who represented the 15th senate district, along with a handful of senators from both parties. They became a powerful voice against the whole idea of the film industry coming to our state. Others joined her with a list of negative commentaries.

"Too expensive for the taxpayers."

"We should bring more traditional jobs; they are steadier."

"The film industry gets tax breaks that other companies don't get."

The constant stream of criticism made producers very nervous about Michigan, but because the incentives were generous, they continued to come.

Shortly after he was elected, Governor Rick Snyder cut tax incentives to the quick and with a snap of the finger, the film industry picked up and left Michigan. The TV series pulled up stakes and left for Chicago the moment they heard about the incentive reductions. Films in the middle of production closed shop and left on a dime, as we had been warned they would.

As I write this, the film industry is essentially gone from Michigan.

The tax incentives could have been decreased in time, if it seemed the right direction, but to cut everything three years after beginning the film industry was too soon. It failed to give the new industry time to grow roots into Michigan's economy. I still strongly believe that diversifying the Michigan economy is a must. Manufacturing, agriculture, film, advanced battery, and renewable energy—we need a sound, enduring economy that will support all these things and last far into the future. We've already made the mistake of relying too heavily on the manufacturing industry. When manufacturing has downturns, the state falls apart. A far more sensible strategy is to bring in every industry possible, *including* manufacturing, so that when manufacturing isn't strong, the other economies keep us afloat.

Mitch Albom never gave up. He lobbied for the continuation of the film industry and even talked to Governor Rick Snyder, but to no avail. The film industry was pushed back— waaaaay back. Right out of the state.

Water issues, the tax drama, media challenges, protecting the health and well being of our constituents, inviting the film industry to Michigan—these were complicated issues and we faced them daily. No matter where we stood on each of these issues, whether we agreed or disagreed, the struggle to help the state come back from the recession joined those in our Democratic caucus together like welded steel. We didn't always agree with one another and often held diametrically opposed views. But despite that, we became a kind of family, and the sweetness of knowing one another, and working together for the greater good, brought with it the sadness of parting.

Chapter XVII

Kate, Bob and Mike

It is February as I write this, and my recovery continues. I hardly ever think of the Chronicle *any more, or my mistakes, or what I could have done differently. I'm in a different phase of my life now. Blessedly.*

But I'm still upset about what our new governor and legislators have done to our state. Not only did they ruin Michigan's blossoming film industry, they upped taxes on working families and seniors. Cuts to schools have been so large that our poorest schools can't even keep their doors open. Government takeovers have put municipalities and school districts under the control of tin pot dictators. Bad legislation is zooming through the legislature like a sled careening down an icy hill.

I've said it before. It's not my individual loss that I'm most concerned about now—it's what is happening in our state. We're in this mess because so many legislators are power hungry. They have chosen to put their own political ambitions ahead of their constituents' concerns; they have given legislators a bad name in our state. But there are some legislators I will never forget. They became my friends and worked with me, side by side, for four years. Kate Ebli, Mike Simpson, and Robert Jones are on that list. Memories of serving with them are the bitter and the sweet.

* * * *

In April 2006, after being on the campaign trail for several months, it occurred to me that though I was with people most of the time—volunteers, campaign staff, potential voters, caucus folks like Lavora Barnes and Mark Fisk, journalists, and photographers—something was missing. I had no one with whom to talk who was doing exactly what I was doing. I was receiving attention and support, yet I longed to have someone to confide in—someone who was having an experience similar to mine.

So I jumped at the chance to attend a candidate training the caucus was conducting. I knew it would be beneficial to my campaign, but I was also hoping to meet candidates that were kindred spirits. The person I remember most from that meeting is Kate Ebli—a tall, big-boned woman, bright, secure about who she was, and brimming with self-confidence. She was so self-assured and smart that initially I was a bit intimidated by her—but I wondered if she might be that kindred spirit I'd been hoping to meet.

I met her again after the election in which we both won our seats, at a woman's caucus held after our caucus retreat at Garland, Michigan, shortly after our official swearing in as State Representatives. Garland is a beautiful retreat center smack dab in the middle of nowhere—near Lewiston, Michigan, in the northeast corner of Michigan's Lower Peninsula. The retreat was enjoyable, informative, and a good chance to get to know my new colleagues. We paid our own way, of course, but it was money well spent. We learned how to run committees, interpret poll results, and communicate our message effectively. We learned what it meant to "hold your powder" (not let people know how you're going to vote).

Mostly, though, we worked on an important part of our job as legislators—building working relationships with colleagues.

Dianne Byrum, former Democratic Leader of the House, hosted the women's caucus at her chalet. And this was where I learned that I didn't need to be intimidated by Kate Ebli. Sure, she was confident, tall, and smart. But her heart was solid gold. Plus, she had a unique sense of humor—she was crack-you-up funny. I remember a lot of laughing at the caucus.

As it turned out, Kate sat behind me during the first term, and I sat behind her during our second term. She loved to tease me about the outrageous things my "friends" in the Republican Party said about me during my first campaign, such as the fact that I had ties to Iraqi terrorists. Because Kate knew I was a speech pathologist and the notion that somehow I had ties to Iraqi terrorists was so absurd, she teased that it must be that I had just been trying to teach the kids how to say Jihad Ji-ji-ji-jihad,"—her way of poking fun at the Republican nonsense.

During the campaign, the Republicans called me the extre-e-e-e-eme Valentine, earning me the nickname of The Extreme Valentine. 2007 was the year we spent many days – and overnights – at the capitol. You can only answer constituents and study issues for so many hours in a row before slap-happiness sets in. Once, in the middle of an all-night session, Kate googled "extreme Valentine." Turns out it is a drink, which consists of some combination of beer, hard alcohol, and Mellow Yellow. Yuck.

Kate and I also sat on the Great Lakes and Environment Committee together our first term, so we joined forces to pass the water legislation that helped to usher in the Water Compact. She also sat on the Energy and Tech Committee, helping me understand the tough energy issues behind the legislation we passed that term, which resulted in a Renewable Portfolio Standard (RPS) for Michigan: 10% clean, renewable energy by the year 2015. The RPS was, in fact, only a small step forward, even though it took an enormous amount of legislative work to create even that. But it was, at least, something.

One of the many things I appreciated about Kate was her willingness to admit she didn't fully understand an issue. One thorny issue we dealt with was—and still is—the formula for Proposal A funding for public schools. She pulled together a small workshop to help us all better understand that convoluted formula and how it affected the schools in our districts.

After she announced she was running for office the first time, an old injury from her airplane-jumping days flared up that made walking difficult for her. It didn't slow her down one bit—she limped from door to door during the campaign, and hobbled around the capitol after she was elected.

One memory of Kate still makes me chuckle to this day. Early in our first term, during a fierce Lansing blizzard, we decided to attend an event at the Beer and Wine Association's headquarters. The weather was terrible and she still wasn't able to walk, so we drove. We pulled out the address, turned on the GPS and started out on our venture. Driving around in circles, miles out of our way, we finally found this elusive spot. Then it took forever to find a parking place, and we had to drive in circles waiting for one to become available. Later, we went to events there on a regular basis—it turns out the place is only two blocks from the Capitol Building. But that day, in a blinding snowstorm, we thought we would never actually get there and find an available parking spot. When I think of the quick walk to Beer and Wine and how often I walked there during my following four years in the capitol, it still brings a smile to my lips.

One day during our second term, I noticed that Kate was wearing a wig. I knew she had recovered from a bout of breast cancer before she ran for office, so I was concerned—but it wasn't something she seemed eager to talk about. I assumed her cancer had returned but said nothing. Later, she decided she couldn't stand the wig and wore scarves instead. Eventually, she discarded the scarves, too. She walked into the chamber day after day tall, confident, and bald—while going through her second bout of chemo for breast cancer. Eventually her hair came back, peach fuzz at first, then a tad longer, finally long enough to be dyed to her usual reddish brown color and restyled. It is one of my most enduring memories of Lansing: the sight of Kate walking into the legislature each day—bald and proud. Now when I think about serving in the state legislature, the first person I picture is Kate Ebli.

One reward of serving in the legislature is the rich tapestry of colleagues you meet and work with: teachers, chemists, CEOs, lawyers, business people, Mary Kay representatives, farmers—the list is endless. Many had years of government service while others were new to the field, as I was. One of the most interesting of these was Bob Jones, former chemist, and also former mayor of Kalamazoo. I met him at State Representative Training, a class Michigan State University offered to new representatives that had started when Michigan's ridiculously short term limits went into effect.

Bob was a quiet man and incredibly bright. Everybody thought of him as his or her best friend, including me. When you'd see Bob around Lansing in the winter, he'd be wearing a leather, cowboy-style hat with a feather hanging from the back and a long leather coat. He had a carefully curled and well-kept handlebar mustache. He was a striking figure in Lansing.

Bob had run for office for the right reason—he wanted to make his community a better place. When he spoke up in caucus, he always had something smart to say, presented with a unique and thoughtful twist. He was quick to take the politics out and discuss what was best for our constituents.

Bob and I came into the legislature in the same class and ran for Senate at the same time. Toward the end of our first term, he announced to our caucus that he had throat cancer and would have to take time away for an operation. He told us a press release to that effect had gone out earlier that day. Bob had the operation and returned to the House healthy and strong a few months later. Toward the end of our second term, though, his voice became weak. That didn't hold him back. If he had something to say, he rose and said it, no matter how squeaky his voice was. And it was always something worth considering.

Mike Simpson also came into the legislature at the same time I did. I first became aware of him on election night, 2006. We were hoping and praying that we Democrats could take at least one of the "Jackson seats." Jackson is a fairly conservative place, the birthplace of the modern Republican Party. So the two Jackson seats generally go Republican. If we were to take the majority, the Democrats needed to win at least one of those seats. Taking both of them was an unexpected and delicious surprise on election night.

Mike Simpson was one of those "Jackson seats," and I've never known a harder-working person. He was known for meeting often with the constituents in the district. Mike would start at one end of his district and work his way to the other end. On the way, he stopped and visited local businesses. One day he walked into a business that was on the verge of closing. He pulled together everyone he could think of, including the governor, to strategize about how they might keep that business open. My understanding was that as a result, 200 jobs were saved.

Mike also heard from a constituent who needed an electric wheelchair. He moved heaven and earth to get that wheelchair. One Republican Rep even sent one of his own constituents to Mike for help with a similar problem. The Republicans weren't shy about doing something like that: appealing to one of us for help, and then bashing us soundly in the press.

Mike and I didn't always agree. During my second term I served on the Agricultural Committee, of which he was the chair. The Farm Bureau wanted to pass some awful legislation to take all livestock regulating out of the hands of local officials and put the state in charge. Republicans, who run as local control candidates, again wanted to take control out of the hands of local officials. It was a power grab, pure and simple. They claimed it was to protect farmers from an extreme Citizen's Initiative being put forth by the Humane Society of the United States (HSUS). The HSUS wanted to stop the practice of "veal crates," "gestation crates," and the practice of squeezing chickens into battery cages.[19] Farmers were claiming that the HSUS legislation would put them out of business.

---

[19] Veal crates are tiny crates baby calves must live in to keep them from moving around, so their meat will be tender. Some claim those crates are cruel. Gestation crate also are tiny crates pigs must live in when they're pregnant so they won't roll over onto their babies when they are born. This issue relates to factory farms, which jam so many animals into small spaces that mother sows rolling over onto their babies becomes a problem. Battery cages jam chickens into a very small space to save money.

I would never want farmers to be put out of business. Farming is the second strongest industry in our state, so of course we want to protect it. But the proposed legislation would have done nothing to protect farmers from the Citizen's Initiative they feared. It just would have taken livestock management out of local control and put it in the hands of the state. The Citizen's Initiative still could have been passed, with or without taking livestock control out of the hands of local officials.

I had many questions about this legislation. I had seen firsthand how damaging it was to take issues such as this out of the hands of local citizens and needed more time to consider it.[20] I begged Mike to wait one more week to bring it up for a vote, but he didn't wait. I believe he was under the spell of Farm Bureau folks, who, by the way, were being dishonest with the farmers and preying on their very real fears.

In the end, when the legislation was brought up for a vote in our committee, I abstained, which greatly irked the Farm Bureau. The legislation passed. Speaker Pro Tem Pam Byrnes didn't bring it up for a vote in the full chamber right away. She got all affected parties together. She'd bring it up for a vote, she said, when those involved could resolve their differences.

Ultimately, the disagreeing parties resolved the issues in a way I could live with. The farmers agreed to make changes

---

[20] One of the first things I worked on as a new legislator was to regulate the sale of fertilizer with phosphates. The phosphates aren't necessary unless it's a new lawn, but phosphate is in all the fertilizer and is destroying our lakes, rivers, and streams. Reasonable solutions could not be enacted locally because of a state law pre-empting local control of this issue. It bugs me that Republicans often run on local control and then pre-empt that control as soon as they have a chance.

in the way they do things over the course of several years, so the HSUS dropped their Citizens' Initiative. I supported the legislation when it came up for a vote on the House floor. In spite of our disagreement on that issue, I had a great deal of respect for Mike's integrity and willingness to work hard to get a job done.

The way Pam Byrnes handled this issue, by the way, made her a bit of a hero to me; she stood her ground until a reasonable compromise was reached. And Speaker Dillon also was a hero, because he didn't interfere with this process, as he could have in his role as speaker.

When we newly elected legislators met for the first time after our campaigns, we compared notes to see who had had the toughest campaigns. Mike's story from the 2006 campaign was by far the worst. He had lost a child to cancer. The day after the funeral, his insurance had been cancelled, and he ended up going into bankruptcy. It's a terrible, but all too familiar, story that many in our country experience—often losing their homes in the process. This was what prompted Mike to run for office. When we compared notes about the ugly campaigns we faced, the story Mike told was the most brutal—that those on the other side of the aisle, the ones who call themselves pro-family, had claimed he was hiding behind the death of a child. Turned my stomach.

Mike was a businessman; he owned a small restaurant in Jackson that shipped in all sorts of delicious food to his campaign headquarters the last weeks of the campaign. The staff talked a great deal about how delicious the food was and how much they appreciated it. Halfway through our second term, though, Mike became seriously ill, and we began to see him in sessions less and less.

What do these three elected state leaders have in common? They all came into office the same year as I did; they all won their seats back in the next election. But before what would have been the beginning of our third term, Kate Ebli, Bob Jones, and Mike Simpson all died. Kate and Bob succumbed to cancer, and Mike Simpson had a massive heart attack. Fourteen percent of our class was gone.

Mike's death was sudden and shocking. I learned about it during a late-night session. The speaker of the House never chaired our sessions; it was always the speaker pro tem— Pam Byrnes, during our second term. But on this night, Speaker Andy Dillon came to the podium. The incessant noise of the chamber slowed. A hush descended. We knew this was serious.

"Our dear friend, Mike Simpson, died of a heart attack earlier today," Speaker Dillon said.

The chamber became deathly silent for many minutes, while we absorbed this news. A time of mourning began. The capitol staff came in, draped a black cloth over Mike's desk, and put a large bouquet of flowers on it (a House tradition when a law-maker dies in office). The seat remains unfilled, with the black cloth draped over it, until the next session. The next representative elected for that seat starts immediately after the fall election, instead of waiting until the first of the year, when others take their seats.

I learned about Bob Jones' death from a text message I received while I was in Fruitport, knocking doors for my Senate campaign. I was deeply saddened, but not surprised. His voice had all but vanished in recent weeks. The black cloth and flowers appeared on Bob's desk as well. Another heartbreaking loss, Bob's death came just a few weeks before the 2010 election.

Kate lost her battle to breast cancer on January 3, 2011, two days after the end of the session. Our mutual friend and colleague, Majority Floor Leader Kathy Angerer had spent much time with Kate in her final days, and had been keeping me informed. She called me on the phone to tell me of Kate's passing. The state flag flew at half-mast in Kate's honor. I still miss Kate deeply—miss our long talks and our shared experiences. I miss being able to tap into her political wisdom.

The job of state representative was a tough one. After three long and mean-spirited campaigns, I sometimes feel fortunate that I came out alive. And I have such deep respect for these three fallen colleagues. I attended each of their funerals and I mourn them to this day. Governor Granholm spoke at Mike's, Speaker Dillon at Bob's, while Kate chose to keep hers more oriented toward family. Her daughter and nieces were the pallbearers, and they all wore tiaras—which Kate always had them do at special family events. Apparently, Kate was always losing earrings, so her sisters wore mismatched earrings in her honor.

Our state lost three magnificent people when it lost Kate, Bob and Mike.[21]

---

[21] We lost other colleagues as well, both before and after my time in the legislature. While I was still running for my first term, the state representative who preceded Kate Ebli, Herb Kehrl, died suddenly while he was still in office. During my first term I served with Aldo Vagnozzi, of the 37th District. After he completed his three terms and was term-limited out (during my second term), he succumbed to cancer. Following my last term, former colleague Judy Nerat, from the Upper Peninsula, lost her battle to cancer. And just recently, Gino Polidori, of Dearborn, lost his battle with cancer. These losses devastated our state as well. Six of us lost our lives. All great people, and all great Democrats.

Chapter XVIII

Deaf Ears

*It's May 2012. I'm at the Louis McMurray Center in Mus-
kegon Heights for a forum about a bill package introduced into
the legislature called "Prevention First." The thrust of the
package is to address the abortion issue from the perspective
of preventing problem pregnancies. Based on the number of
people streaming into the room, this is clearly an issue vital to
the women in this community.*

*While I was in politics, my opponents often portrayed me
as a cruel, heartless woman who didn't care about babies. I
was castigated, insulted, and yelled at for my position on
abortion. It was painful—having people twist the truth of who
you are and what you believe. Still, it's part of running for
office. The hurt has faded, though I'm glad to no longer have to
deal with being misrepresented.*

*This forum is taking me back to the "pro-choice" vs. "pro-
life" issue that I faced constantly—both as a candidate and as
a legislator.*

* * * *

"Everyone must pick a side," Mark Fisk told me early in
my first campaign. "You can be pro-choice or pro-life, but you
must choose one side or the other."

This advice reflects Lansing's deep divide on the issue of abortion. The two sides are always lined up against each other, and always ready for battle—there is no such thing as a middle ground. This all-or-nothing thinking is not only a ridiculous way to solve problems, it's also tearing our nation apart. It didn't feel right to me when Mark Fisk said it, and it doesn't feel right to me now. That's why I declined both the "pro-life" and "pro-choice" labels and instead called my position "pro-solution."

The plain truth is that this issue isn't about "choice" or "life." It isn't about whether anyone is for abortion or against it. Those who call themselves pro-life seem to think abortions will magically disappear if legal access is denied. That's ridiculous, of course—the fact is that, legal or not, women will have them—as they have since the beginning of time. It's just that if they are legal, women won't die in the process. Clearly, a far more effective strategy to stop abortions is to provide birth control, which is exactly what the pro-choice folks want. So what in the world are we arguing about?

In my view, we have a problem. We need to stop arguing about it, throw the labels out, and find effective solutions. That's why I call myself "pro-solution" rather than pro-life or pro-choice.

Maybe instead of spending hundreds of millions of dollars fighting each other, we should seek solutions through medical science, so that no one ever again will have to make the terrible decision of choosing between a mother's well being and a baby's. Maybe by working together, we could even tackle the thorny issues of rape and incest. The truth is that until we find solutions the two sides can agree on, many serious problems will remain unresolved—to the detriment of every last person in this country. Education in high poverty areas, our country's high infant mortality rate, contaminated air and water, and global climate change are examples of the problems that never will find solutions until we resolve the abortion issue. Sadly, many voters won't even discuss finding effective solutions to those critical problems until we come to an agreement about reproductive justice.

"Let's stop arguing and find common ground," I said to deaf ears, for all the years I was in the legislature. I do truly believe that a middle ground exists, and that we should work harder to find it. Interestingly, when I described what that meant, the pro-choice groups embraced me and the pro-life groups labeled me a baby-killer. If you want the vote of pro-life people, you must use their exact terminology—with no room for thought or nuance. You are either pro-life or an evil baby killer.

Frankly, I'm convinced that dirty energy, big coal, and big oil love this endless arguing and are taking advantage of well-meaning people to keep it alive. Pro-life legislators are usually the same legislators who support the dirty coal and oil industries, keeping them active at a time we should be moving toward clean, renewable, life-enhancing energy. As long as big coal and big oil can keep pro-life voters support-ing Republicans, they never will have to worry about their industries dying a natural death and going the way of the buggy whip.

I'm troubled when people say they would never vote for a Democrat because of the abortion issue. For one thing, it simply isn't true. Many Democrats take on the pro-life label and vote accordingly. For another thing, people who claim this label often vote against other life-enhancing measures: finding clean energy sources, seeking measures to decrease our high infant mortality rate, and investing in programs that will decrease crime. They're not so much pro-life as they are pro-criminalizing abortion.

According to the Guttmacher Institute (an organization advancing sexual reproductive health worldwide through research, policy analysis, and public education) in conjunction with the World Health Organization, the countries with the most restrictive abortion laws also have the highest rate of abortions. Those with solid access to birth control and sex education have a lower abortion rate.[22]

It should be clear by now that restrictive abortion laws, while they may cause people to feel empowered, really aren't effective at limiting abortions. There isn't one iota of doubt in my mind that we'll never achieve the goal of fewer abortions simply by reducing legal access. Instead, women of all ages will act from fear and resort to back alley abortions: unsafe, unhealthy, and deadly. In addition, issues of rape, incest, and the health and life of the mother remain unresolved.

I sometimes wonder if those who call themselves pro-life really have thought through the logic of their position. What would really happen if having an abortion were a crime? Would a woman seeking to terminate her pregnancy be thrown into prison? What if she had other children? Would those children be raised without a mother? Or would we need prisons with accommodations for children?

What about pregnant 13-year-olds? Or 11-year-olds? Or nine-year-olds? As much as no one wants this to be a reality, it is. It's an ugly truth that children do get pregnant—most often, through rape and incest. Do we really want a distant legislator to make a decision about that child's well being? Obviously, something is drastically wrong when a nine-year-old gets pregnant; it's likely she's being sexually abused. Those who call themselves pro-life seem to think that if that

---

[22] More information about this is available on the Guttmacher Institute Web site in the article, "Facts on Induced Abortion Worldwide."

girl gets an abortion, the abuse is pushed under the rug and she can go right back into the same situation. This is clearly unacceptable any way you look at it. Of course, whatever plan is decided upon, that pregnant child must be cared for. This includes ensuring she is safe from sexual abuse, with a healthy plan for her future. But it also seems clear that the decision is best left in the hands of those who know the child—not in the hands of a distant legislator who knows nothing about her.

Working toward criminalizing abortion has had many damaging side effects for state governments. In their zeal to restrict abortion rights, state legislatures across the country are promoting further regulation of miscarriages to ensure abortions aren't hidden under the guise of miscarriages. What a terrible idea! After the birth of my first child, I had two devastating miscarriages. Both were heart-wrenching losses I wouldn't wish on anyone. Those seeking restrictive abortion measures want to make that experience worse by bringing in the law and enforcing investigations. I can't imagine how awful it would have been to have someone snooping into my personal medical situation at that difficult, vulnerable time in my life. Any woman who has ever experienced a miscarriage, and there are many of us, would certainly agree with me.

I know that thousands of people believe deep in their hearts that abortion is murder. Heartfelt and sincere in this belief, they're deeply troubled by legal abortions. Surely most of these people could come to understand that criminalizing abortions won't stop them. Preventing problem pregnancies makes so much more common sense. Sadly, though, the pro-life movement has become filled with extreme and illogical zealots who, while they vilify abortions, want to eliminate the most effective solution to prevent them: birth control.

After four years in the legislature, I have come to realize that the pro-life movement is at least as responsible for the high rate of abortion in the United States as is the pro-choice movement. It's like the story of Romeo and Juliet. The two families fought against each other with such vehemence that in the end, their children died. We are fighting with such intensity about the issue of abortion that the number of abortions is going up. Along the way, our healthcare issues go unresolved, our air causes young people to have asthma, and too many of those living in poverty end up in prison rather than in college. Too many won't address these issues while abortions stay legal.

In Lansing, it seemed to me that when an issue came up related to adoption, birth control, or abortion, legislators with right-to-life endorsements would immediately to Ed Rivet, Right-to-Life lobbyist, to ask him how they could vote. I have deep respect for Ed Rivet, but I wish legislators were more capable of thinking for themselves. It gives Right to Life enormous power in the state of Michigan—which, in my opinion, they haven't always used wisely.

I brought my belief in finding common ground between the two sides of this debate to my job as chair of the Family and Children Services Committee during my second term in the legislature. The results were unexpected. I had decided that if Michigan Right to Life promoted any issue with which I agreed, I would jump right on it and work to get it passed. I hoped it would convince those on both sides that I was committed to bridging the divide. That was my thinking the day I was sitting at my desk in the House chamber when I received a note from Right to Life lobbyist Ed Rivet, asking me to meet with him in the lobby. Out into the lobby I went, eager to meet this controversial Lansing icon. Ed, legislative director of Right to Life since 1988, is a short, intense man and takes his job seriously.

I introduced myself and said, "I'm glad to finally meet you."

"I'm glad to meet you, too," he replied. "I'd like to talk to you about a bill that is now in the Family and Children Services Committee."

The bill in question, originally introduced by Alpena Representative Matt Gillard at the request of a young woman whose parents had recently adopted a baby, would allow adoptive parents to have the same right to childcare leave that other parents have. She didn't think it was fair that her parents were denied childcare leave because they had adopted their baby rather than giving birth to him.

"I'm hoping you will pick this bill up in your committee," he told me.

I told him then and there that I agreed with the bill 100%.

Soon afterward, I brought the bill up, and after a few compromises, it zoomed through committee. More important, an unlikely relationship developed between myself, labeled pro-choice by the Lansing establishment, and pro-life Ed Rivet. Later, we worked on another piece of legislation—this one far more controversial. During my second year as chair, Representative Lesia Liss introduced a bill to allow adult adoptees access to their own original birth certificates (OBC). Sounds simple, doesn't it? But as it turns out, nothing in Lansing is ever easy. I called a Family and Children's Services committee meeting to discuss this bill. After winding my way through the maze of the third-floor committee rooms to the small room where this committee met, I called the meeting to order, pounded the large gavel, accepted a motion to receive the minutes from our last meeting, and introduced the bill to allow adult adoptees access to their own original birth certificates.

The basic problem related to adult adoptees gaining access to their own OBCs is the confusing network of legislation that started in 1945. At that time, illegitimate babies' birth certificates were stamped just that: illegitimate, which social workers realized would cause great damage to the innocent baby. At that time, adoptions also dramatically increased, and there was concern that the moms who released their babies for adoption might try to search for those babies, disrupting them in their new families. So a law was passed to seal the OBC, and issue a new birth certificate at the time of the adoption. Only a judge could rule to unseal the OBC. This all changed in 1981, when the law was updated. After that, an adult adoptee could have access to his or her own OBC at the age of 18 or older, under certain circumstances. This complex and confusing situation left a hole in our law—and in the hearts of Michigan adult adoptees—which some in our committee were determined to correct.

Let's be clear. The 1945 law was put into place to protect the baby, not to protect the identity of the birth mother. They did it so the mother wouldn't be able to find her baby (now part of an adopted family) and to prevent the possibility of the child seeing the word "illegitimate" stamped on his or her birth certificate. That was 69 years ago. No one stamps "illegitimate" on anyone's birth certificate anymore. In 1981, the law changed, and records are now open except when the parents of birth deny all access, which is exceedingly rare. The dilemma is that those born and adopted between 1945 and 1981 are caught in a kind of limbo, and can't have access to their own OBCs without a court order. Testimony from several experts set the stage for what was to follow.

"If you take yourself back to the fifties and sixties," experts testified, "you will remember that when these adoptions took place, unwed pregnancies were veiled in shame and secrecy. The girl was whisked away until the baby was born, released the child for adoption, then returned to her life as though nothing had happened."

It seems obvious that we should just allow the adult adoptees the access to their OBCs that they crave. Why not? But many were concerned about the anonymity of the women who released them for adoption. This is where things get really complicated, due to a decades-long misunderstanding of the original law. Many social workers, in their zeal to promote adoption (which they thought was better for the child), began promising anonymity. "No one will be able to come and disrupt your future life," they falsely promised.

As a result of this promise, some began to believe the legislation was put in place to protect the mother who had released her child for adoption. Nothing could be further from the truth. The fact is that during that time, no one gave a hoot about the woman who actually gave birth to the child— her family and community viewed her with contempt. Absolutely nothing ever was done to protect her from anything or anyone. This is a terrible truth, and blessedly, our society has moved passed this disparaging attitude. Clearly, the reissued birth certificate has nothing to do with the woman who gave birth to the child. It was enacted to protect the *adoptive* parents.

Adult adoptees, meanwhile, often have a real need to see their original birth certificates—it completes their identity. In a growing number of states, adult adoptees walk in and get their own OBCs, no questions asked. But adult adoptees born between 1945 and 1981 in Michigan can't get access without a judge's permission. It's a heartbreaking situation, because too often the judge simply won't give permission. And many adult adoptees feel degraded by having to ask permission for something as basic as a birth certificate. This is why the bill originated. Adult adoptees were seeking the right to obtain their OBCs without the permission of a judge. To add to the confusion, with the advent of the Internet, adult adoptees often find their parents of birth—with or without their OBCs. And those who already have found their parents of birth *still* can't have access to their own OBCs—even when withholding those OBCs serves no purpose. When introduced to this situation, I didn't have a personal understanding of the issues involved—but the job of a legislator is to listen to constituents and make decisions based on *their* needs. Listening to adult adoptees convinced me this isn't a trivial issue for them.

As I listened carefully to the many adult adoptees testifying in committee, I eventually understood their pain at being denied their OBCs. I also understood their pain at continually being referred to as adopted children. "Please don't call us children," many of them requested. "We aren't children; we are adults and want to be treated as such. Please call us adult adoptees."

Nor is it trivial for the mother who gave birth to the child.

During the fifties and sixties, deep shame affected these young women who had become pregnant. Generally, these young women didn't have an opportunity to discuss the adoption process or resolve any uncertainty. The baby was taken after birth, the mothers signed releases under duress, and their lives continued. But consistently, these women carry the shame of their out-of-wedlock births with them for their entire lives. Over and over again, when women who released a child for adoption reconnected with that child (now an adult), the shame evaporated. Many women reported this phenomenon, whether they wanted to be contacted by their children or not.

"When I met my child, the shame I had carried with me was finally released. The relief was huge and unexpected."

This is the sort of comment we heard repeatedly in committee hearings—and we received many more letters and calls from women with the same story. I honestly felt that those who fought this OBC legislation did so out of a misguided attempt to protect the birth mothers. Instead, in my opinion, they were keeping those women locked in their original shame. These women aren't weak or vulnerable; they haven't been abused and beaten down. They simply live with a terrible chapter in their lives that remains buried due to misguided legislation that keeps secrets hidden and shame locked in.

Could I promise that women who had released children for adoption wouldn't face some disruption in their lives if they met those birth children? Of course not. But I could promise that thousands of adults were suffering because of the law as it was, and is now, written. And written into the legislation we were trying to pass was every protection we could possibly offer to the mothers who gave birth, while still maintaining dignity for the adult adoptees.

The pro-life and pro-choice legislators, from what I could tell, rarely agreed on anything. But sadly, they agreed on this one thing: OBCs should remain locked away from adult adoptees. It's an old opinion based on old attitudes and fears, and no one has questioned or analyzed it for decades. Many minds were locked shut on the issue, and no amount of information could pry them open. Toward the end, there was slight movement on the pro-choice side, in that the National Organization of Women lobbyist understood the shame aspect and realized how unhealthy that was for the women they were trying to protect.

But all Republicans on the committee, as well as one conservative Democrat, opposed this legislation. I did my best to educate them by providing books, information, films, and committee testimony—everything I could think of, to encourage them to reconsider. I think the material I provided remained unopened. Minds were already made up and remained shut, and as a result, the legislation never got out of committee. Representatives Lesia Liss, Dian Slavens, Jimmy Womack, and myself valiantly supported the adult adoptees' efforts to change the law, but to no avail. As a result, adult adoptees continue to struggle needlessly with this issue in Michigan.

This issue shows how term limits clearly hamper growth. As I reviewed the process in my mind, I realized a different approach might have been more successful. I simply didn't have the experience to launch a different strategy at that point in my career. We need experienced legislators, which simply don't exist in Lansing anymore.

And who worked most diligently to fight this battle with me? Ed Rivet, the Right-To-Life lobbyist. This is a perfect example of the statement: *Politics makes for strange bedfellows.* In previous legislatures he was against the legislation, but he did the most unlikely thing—he listened to the testimony in committee, studied what other states were doing, and changed his mind. He then further researched the bill's history and came to believe what I did—that too many people were being deeply hurt by this law and no one had anything to gain by it.

Working with someone across ideological lines branded me as a traitor to some. Distrust is high among people who have struggled for many years and faced constant betrayal and frustration, and they couldn't understand how I could ever team up with Ed Rivet. If he was for it, I think they believed, it must be wrong.

After my term had ended, I teamed up with Ed Rivet again in an effort to keep the Catherine Ferguson School open. Part of the Detroit Public Schools, it's a wonderful school for teen girls raising their own children. Ultimately, the school was kept open as a charter school operated by the Blanche Kelso Bruce Academy.[23]

I truly hope that one day, we'll stop fighting about abortion and find common ground. Reasonable solutions are possible. Even after four years in a legislature where everyone else was either pro-choice or pro-life, I still consider myself pro-solution. And I keep shouting about it—right straight into the wind.

---

[23] I'm sorry to report that this once fine school has failed to provide students the quality of education they deserve, which has resulted in a lawsuit, according to the June 5, 2013, edition of Eclectablog.

Chapter XIX

Rodents in Houghton Lake and Other Surprises

Today on Morning Joe *I heard Joe Scarborough say that he loved every minute of his time in Congress and misses it every day. I don't often agree with Mr. Scarborough, but on that remark, I agree 100%. Those memories are my fondest and richest, and I feel blessed beyond measure to have had the opportunity to serve.*

Reading through past journal posts makes me realize that many of the emotions that plagued me after my Senate race defeat are fading, as I knew they would. Sometimes it truly is just a matter of waiting things out. I've noticed the same healing among others who have lost races that were important to them. Some keep their time of bitterness to themselves, some are more open about it, but it always seems to pass. I am glad.

My precious memories of running for office and serving in the legislature seem vibrant and real, even more so now that the pain of my defeat is being replaced with memories of joy and friendship. And, of course, I still have many memories of the fascinating challenges of creating public policy.

* * * *

When Majority Floor Leader (MFL) Steve Tobocman went to Alpena, Matt Gillard's district, to knock on doors with him, Matt warned Steve about some hot-button local issues. One of them was Road Ends, but apparently Matt didn't pronounce it clearly.

"People are very concerned about road ends up here," Matt explained to Steve. "You're going to get a lot of questions about it."

"Rodents?" Steve thought to himself. "Rodents are a problem in Alpena?"

But no, rodents aren't a problem in Matt's district. It's road ends.

In fact, a great deal of controversy arose related to the issue of what to do with a road that ended at the edge of Houghton Lake in Roscommon County in the northern Lower Peninsula. During the few weeks this issue dominated the conversation in Lansing, the terms "front-lotters," "back-lotters," and "lake access" became part of the vernacular and could be heard floating in the air anywhere legislators and lobbyists gathered—in the lobby outside the chamber, at noontime fundraisers, and during evening receptions.

This is a good place to mention a question I often get asked: Does it do any good to write a letter to one's legislator when concerned about an issue?

The answer is yes.

And this was one case where a letter from a constituent clarified a muddy issue for me and was the deciding factor in my vote (on the side of the back-lotters). I can honestly say that I didn't make decisions based on who was sweet-talking me or paying for my lunch. I sought out information about how a decision would impact my own constituents or citizens across the state. The volume of constituents concerned about an issue, added to information I garnered from committee reports as well as who supported a bill, were most likely to impact my vote. This time, though, after my research left me undecided, it was a heartfelt letter that made all the difference.

The issue of road ends had been brewing for many years around Houghton Lake, but because a local compromise couldn't be reached, the issue ended up at the State House. The front-lotters lived right on the lake, and generally weren't year-round residents. They lived downstate nine months of the year, and came to Houghton Lake for the summer months. Back-lotters lived on the lake year-round, and considered themselves the caretakers of the water when the front-lotters were absent. These back-lotters had access to the lake during the summer months by way of the road ends. I wasn't surprised to hear that these residents used the lakeshore as a swimming beach at the road end. But I was surprised to learn about the extensive array of docks and boat slips where the road ended at the lake. The front-lotters found this a nuisance and wanted the docks down. The back-lotters had been using those docks for generations, and didn't think it was fair to be forced to take their docks down when they were the ones who looked after the lake year-round.

That was the situation, as I knew it, when I received a heartfelt, handwritten letter from a long-time resident of Houghton Lake. She explained that the back-lotters had always had access to the lake during the summer months, and had built docks and boat slips there. Front-lotters and back-lotters had been friends, and had shared the lake with one another for many generations. In recent years, though, the front-lotters had become possessive of the lake and wanted the back-lotters out of the road ends. This meant no docks, boat slips, or swimming beach. This just didn't seem fair to her. The back-lotters lived there, and wanted summer access to their own jewel of a lake. They were willing to compromise, but didn't want to be thrown off the property.

In my view, Representative Matt Gillard did excellent legislative work with this issue, working with all sides to come up with a fair and reasonable compromise. All parties couldn't agree, though, which caused dissension when his compromise came up for a vote. House Bills 4463 and 4464 passed through the House of Representatives in July 2007.

The bill never passed through the Senate. In 2012, a bill related to Road Ends, SB778, passed into law. With the legislature under the complete control of Republicans, no compromise was necessary.

Matt Gillard's good work on the road ends issue was a good example of a legislator's constant need to find middle ground. Another example was the smoking ban—or, more correctly, smoke-free workplace legislation. This issue first arose in Commerce Committee, on which I served during my first term. We heard from doctors about all the poisons in tobacco, and we heard from musicians whose friends had died young because the only place they could ply their trade was in smoke-filled bars. Michigan was, in fact, one of the last states to enact such a law. We also learned that the death rate from heart attacks had shrunk dramatically in smoke-free states, which in itself was a convincing reason to change the law in Michigan. By far the most compelling testimony I heard was from a woman whose sister had died due to second-hand smoke. The woman testifying was a lawyer and really knew how to put her argument together. If there was ever doubt in my mind about providing clear air to workers, her testimony removed that doubt.

Her sister never had smoked a day in her life, but to pursue her career in writing, had found it necessary to constantly enter areas where she was inundated with second-hand smoke. Her eventual diagnosis was a type of cancer associated with second-hand smoke, and she died a terrible death while one of her teen-aged sons looked on.

In fact, my constituents were begging me to support the smoking ban. It seemed that all anyone needed to do was whisper the words "smoking ban" in a back room somewhere, and my phone messages and inbox were filled with requests to enact it. And at every family reunion I attended, a few people would ask me what was taking Michigan so long to enact that law. Even my business-loving, Republican relatives were becoming disgusted by the legislature's lack of action on this issue. They wanted to be able to take their children out to dinner with the family without worrying about second-hand smoke. "Get your party on board!" I wanted to retort. Instead, I smiled and suggested they contact their (Republican) legislator about the matter.

One stumbling block was the Detroit casinos. They were in competition with Indian casinos, which didn't have to go smoke free because they aren't bound by Michigan laws. The Detroit casinos were convinced a smoking ban on their gaming floors would destroy their business. With the tremendous jobs loss Detroit had already experienced, the Detroit legislators were terrified of the casinos closing down. This caused some crumbling on the edges of our caucus. Republicans were no help, of course. It almost seemed like if a bar or restaurant owner lost a customer somewhere, now *that* was a disaster. But people dying from the effects of second-hand smoke didn't seem to matter as much. It was frustrating that the newspapers tended to blame the Detroit legislators and let the Republicans off the hook. I'm not sure why they did this—except that maybe everyone had become accustomed to the fact that Republican legislators are there to work for businesses, rather than citizens. Everyone expected the Democrats to carry the bill, so when some of them bailed, the press blamed them, rather than the Republicans who also opposed the bill. (I don't see how this lack of concern about the lives of workers and citizens computes with so-called Republican allegiance to the concept of pro-life—just one of many inconsistencies between their policies and their talking points.)

During my second term, Representative Joan Bauer of Lansing, who represented the 68th District, took the lead in making sure the smoking ban legislation came up for a vote. Early in the term, which started in January 2009, leadership had promised they would deal with this issue in the spring. By November, we realized this was nothing more than a stalling tactic. Without action, the bill would lie dormant for yet another term.[24]

"Let's have a press conference on the front steps of the capital," Joan suggested, "calling for elected leaders to bring this up for a vote."

The small coalition of supporters actively working on this bill agreed, and suggested a deadline for its resolution—or else the press conference. So we gave House leaders a deadline: *By such-and-such a date, if we have not resolved this issue, we'll talk about it to the press on the front steps of the capital.* Much to our consternation, House leadership kept putting us off and pushing the deadline back. The coalition pushed Joan, she pushed leadership, and the lobbyist pushed anybody who needed it. Periodically, the whips would

---

[24] I came to realize that this stalling tactic was often used to defeat legislation that was excellent public policy but difficult to pass. The tactic usually is accompanied by a slap on the back and assurances that we all want the same thing here, we just need patience.

come around and ask what version of the smoking ban we would support. My answer was consistent: "Whatever we need to do to get this passed, count me in."

In the end, we reached a compromise. Casinos were exempted only on their gaming floors, not in the restaurants. The bills were passed into law in December 2009, and the law was enacted in May 2010. I was proud of Andy Dillon and our leadership, along with the Republican leadership, for their work on this intractable, but important, piece of legislation. There was some fallout, particularly in bars that don't also serve food. But heart-attack deaths in Michigan have fallen. I know this has been extremely frustrating for some businesses, and I truly hope they'll find a way to make a good livelihood even with the smoke-free workplace law in place. Or maybe they will be the buggy-whip businesses of this generation and adjust their operations accordingly. Change is hard. Sometimes, though, it's necessary.

The fight for smoke-free workplace legislation was long and arduous, but not nearly as colorful as the fight for helmet-free motorcycles. The group "American Bikers Aiming Toward Education" (ABATE) was the main supporter of repealing Michigan's law requiring motorcycle riders to wear helmets. When they came to Lansing to advocate for their cause, everyone knew they were there. Tattoos and piercings were de rigueur, and clothing was either battered denim or leather. Most of the bikers, men and women alike, had ponytails and fascinating jewelry—long earrings and chain necklaces. Many of the men had long, pointy beards. They certainly were a stark contrast to typical Lansing business wear.

I liked the ABATE people. I appreciated their enthusiasm and individuality. But I didn't agree with them—then or now. Statistics are clear: Without helmets, more motorcyclists will die or experience serious injury. Police departments and medical personnel stood firmly against repealing the helmet law, because before it went into place they had seen the results daily in emergency rooms and morgues across the state. In 2008, while I was still serving, the law made it through both chambers—only to be vetoed by Governor Granholm.

This has all changed now. On April 12, 2012, the legislature repealed the law to require motorcycle riders to wear helmets, so bikers now can go helmet-free in certain circumstances.

Every day, I see motorcyclists riding around town without their helmets, inviting disaster. According to a *Motorcycle USA* article by Associate Editor Byron Wilson, Assistant Research Scientist, Carol Flannagan, of the University of Michigan's Transportation Research Institute (UMTRI) conducted an initial study of crash data from 2012 related to the repeal of Michigan's helmet law. Factoring alcohol and other risk factors out, Flannagan found that, according to crash reports between April 13 and December 3, 2012, riders not wearing a helmet were twice as likely as helmeted riders to die in a crash, and faced 60% more risk of sustaining serious injury. I'm glad the repeal didn't happen under my watch. It took a so-called pro-life legislature and governor to make that happen.

One unmitigated disaster did occur under my watch. It was, in my opinion, the big kahuna of all legislative blunders—the Michigan Business Tax (MBT). To better explain this story, I must delve back into the fascinating history of tax policy. Please try to wade through the potential boredom—the history of tax policy is crucial to the story.

In 1975, Michigan enacted the Single Business Tax (SBT), which was intended to simplify business taxes by consolidating them into one tax. But by 2006, the tax was universally hated by all businesses and repealed. When I came into office, Michigan's budget not only faced a $1.8 billion hole because of the income tax cuts—along with the fall of the auto industry—it also now faced an additional $1.8 billion hole because of the SBT's demise. Do the math: that is a hole of $3.6 billion. After many years of cuts to services, that would have been an additional $3.6 billion more in cuts. As usual, Democrats and Republicans didn't look at this the same way. Republicans thought those cuts would be good; Democrats worried about the services that would have to be cut. The major flaw of the SBT, in my view, was that it taxed gross receipts. A business that bought paint to sell was taxed not only on the profit, but on the cost of the paint, too. This just wasn't fair—it wasn't surprising that businesses hated it.

After Governor Granholm was elected, she agreed that the SBT should be changed, but she wanted a replacement that was revenue neutral. The Chamber of Commerce didn't want a replacement; they just wanted it gone. That is precisely what happened. They found a way to repeal the SBT. But when we Democrats came in, we wanted to continue funding education, public safety, and public health, along with a host of other services, so we looked for a revenue neutral solution.

"Go to the businesses," Speaker Dillon said. "Find out what they want and need in a business tax." I don't always agree with Andy Dillon, but that, in my view, was brilliant leadership.

State Representatives Paul Condino and Steve Bieda did just that. They studied the issue, talking to business leaders to find out what they needed. They also researched taxes in other states that had been effective. After months of work, they came up with a plan that had been highly effective in other states and had actually spurred job growth. Businesses that create jobs here would have a break; those that don't, would pay more. The bill that left the House of Representatives taxed the profit margin, not the gross receipts.

It was brought up for a vote in the House at a late-night session. The governor was there. The entire chamber stood and watched as the representatives voted and their names came up on the voting board. Some Democrats voted yes, and their names turned green immediately. Some Republicans voted no, and their names turned red immediately. Many from both sides of the aisle stayed off the board, so their names stayed orange. Those legislators were the center of attention. Legislators and the governor talked with them—answering questions, giving information, twisting arms, and urging more green votes. Eventually, green won out, and the bill passed through the House of Representatives. It looked like middle ground was established, and a solution was emerging. It would take months to print up the new forms, so this wasn't something that could be put on the back burner for several months. Out of necessity, it went right straight to the Senate.

And the Senate is where the bill fell apart, in my opinion. In the end, according to my understanding, the chair of Tax Policy refused to bring it up for a vote in her committee without the gross receipts piece being added back in. The Senate committee made other changes as well, taking away the bill's effectiveness for spurring job growth. At the end of the day, that mess of a bill passed into law and, voila! We went from the much-hated SBT to the much-hated MBT. My extensive research didn't reveal the even bigger mess it would eventually become, so I supported it. Businesses hated it, which should have brought about instant revision. But we were back to the same spot: Democrats wanted it revenue neutral, and Republicans wanted to throw the whole thing out. We remained stuck in that limbo until the Republicans took over the legislature in 2011.

At that point, the legislature threw out the bill in favor of a straight 6% business tax, as well as a tax on seniors, a repeal of the earned income tax credit (EITC) for working families, and massive cuts to public services. It was a tax shift that put less burden on the 1% and greater burden on the 99%.

In retrospect, I can say that the Senate stymied pretty much everything I came to Lansing to do: put ground water in the public trust, repeal the complete immunity that Michigan, and Michigan alone, gives to drug companies, and put an end to out-of-state trash. In addition, I'm a big believer in getting as many people as possible to vote, so I thought we needed no-reason absentee voting, which the Senate also wouldn't support. That's why I decided to take a crack at running for the state senate myself. I thought I knew what I was getting into.

Many surprises lay ahead.

Chapter XX

More Thoughts on My Senate Race: High Points, Low Points, and a Few Thank Yous

It's now a year and a half since my failed campaign for the state Senate. As I take my seat at my favorite café, I recall a recent edition of the Melissa Harris-Perry Show in which she discussed losing presidential candidates with Scott Farris, author of the book, Almost President. *Farris pointed out that, at least in presidential politics, losers often have held the key to profound societal transformation. According to The Honorable David Abshire, former Ambassador to NATO, Farris's work "reassures us all that even out of bitter campaigns and defeats, losers do come back and contribute profoundly to major realignments, decency, and equality in American politics." As a person recovering from a defeat, I am heartened by these words and Mr. Farris's work. Maybe there is a spot for me yet in the political landscape of Michigan and its 34th Senate district.*

The Senate campaign was fraught with difficulties, though. Recreating it has been the toughest part of writing this political memoir. Perhaps that's why I needed to begin with it—to put it out there and then move backward, to my victories. Now my memoir has come full circle, and I'm back to the months preceding my defeat.

When Goeff Hansen won the seat, I congratulated him according to custom. He had won decisively and now had the huge responsibility of representing his district. I support him in that important work. But now, it's important for me to take up the job of the losing candidate. This is both to be exceedingly honest about the experience of the campaign, and clear about my judgment concerning the work of the person now holding that seat.

The line between telling the bold truth and being a sore loser, though, is razor thin. That's the line I'm trying to walk, with integrity and truthfulness. It's not easy.

* * * *

Lows: Other 2010 Legislature Losses

The initial response to my decision to run for Senate was a heady experience. People all over Lansing began referring to me as Senator Valentine once I announced my intentions. I immediately felt part of a collective political effort to make improvements in our state government.

But it was not to be. Instead, in 2010, I became a member of the "kicked-out caucus." I wasn't alone. Along with Representative Kate Ebli, who coined the phrase, Representative Kathleen Law also lost her Senate bid. Kathleen, a chemist by training, understands better than most the importance of clean air and water. As a result, she was determined to bring renewable energy to Michigan; in fact, she was the first legislator in the country to introduce Feed-In Tariffs—a policy mechanism, popular in Germany, which helps owners of renewable-energy equipment gain a liberal share of their equipment investment by offering them long-term contracts that enable them to earn a share of the profit for the energy they produce. Kathleen continues to work toward a cleaner environment in Michigan, even though she's no longer in the legislature.

Another huge loss in the House was Representative Jennifer Haase, former teacher and top-notch legislator. She was, and still is, dedicated to education in Michigan and to the many students she served through the years. She worked harder than any legislator I know to bring good legislation to our state and to get re-elected so that her work could continue. She was replaced by 23-year-old Republican Anderea LaFontaine, a longtime waitress at Ken's Country Kitchen in Richmond (according to *Wikipedia*).

My husband Phil on the left, Sharon Polidon on the right and Iin the middle – at the announcement for Senate at the Margaret Drake Elliot Park in Muskegon.

Even Representative Jeff Mayes, one of the most conservative Democrats in the House of Representatives, who did an excellent job representing his conservative district, lost his bid for Senate. 2010 was a tough year to be a Democrat in Michigan—or anywhere else, for that matter. In the kicked-out caucus, I was in good company.

Like my campaigns for state representative, my senate race was a roller coaster ride, with unexpected highs and plenty of crashing to the ground. There were the photo shoots, with their accompanying wardrobe changes and efforts to look natural and relaxed in front of the camera (still challenging for me), the house parties, the fundraisers, the doors to be knocked on again and again, and the endless fundraising calls—all of the nitty-gritty of a serious campaign—exhausting, gratifying, and frustrating.

An additional dimension was that I looked forward to working in the African-American community. As I mentioned in Chapter 2, I came of age when the Jim Crow (segregation) laws of the south were, at long last, ending. Freedom riders traveled throughout the South, challenging the "whites only" signs that came with the laws of segregation. The courage of these activists made an indelible impression on me. I regretted being too young to be a freedom rider myself.

In fact, my interest in the civil rights issue prompted me to take a class in African-American History at Grand Rapids Community College in 1969. Before taking that class, I was unbelievably naïve and ignorant about African-American history. The college class opened my eyes to what it really meant to be a slave in the south—far from the sanitized version in our high school history classes. The books and writings that we studied created a devastating picture of life as a slave—families torn apart, daily rapes and murder, torture and persecution.

We also learned about the Jim Crow south, as well as the "separate but equal" laws—they may have been separate but were never equal. Our African-American population was systematically marginalized and often denied the rights of citizenship. Sometime in the early 2000s, I became involved in the Institute for Healing Racism, a class offered to residents of Muskegon County and led by Gordon Rinard, a local civil rights activist. After my experience with the Institute, I studied and read everything I could get my hands on related to African-American history. That history is something we're still learning to deal with today as a society. I've always wanted to be part of the solution and saw the senate campaign as one possible avenue toward engaging in that prcess.

During the campaign, I spent a good deal of time in the African-American community—attending churches, knocking on doors, walking in parades, and learning about challenges and concerns. Through these experiences, I learned a lot. Mostly, though, I just met a lot of wonderful people and created memories I will always treasure. Campaign worker and friend Trill Bates was key to our work in the African-American community. The most thorough door knocker I ever encountered in my years of canvassing, she stayed out every day until she had knocked on every last door on her list. She also arranged for me to attend and speak at a variety of church services and events in Muskegon's African-American community.

I learned that European and African-American religious traditions are very different. European-American church services run by the clock: If the service begins at 10:00 and if it's not over by 11:00, parishioners complain. In addition, European-American religious services are for the most part quiet and reverent. African-American services, on the other hand, are filled with joy and enthusiasm. They are cathartic

Me, Trill, friend and campaign worker, Anne Pawli, staffer, and Nana Kratochvil, president of the Progressive Democratic Women's Caucus.

in nature; the gospel music pulls you out of your seat and you can't help but sway to the rhythm of the songs. Services, not particularly held to any schedule, operate by God's time, and God doesn't own a wrist-watch. Services can last up to two—or sometimes even three—hours. I found the time went quickly, though, because of the rich musical experience. Apparently, it's not uncommon for politicians to attend African-American churches, talk to the congregation, and leave the building before services are over. Not me. I wouldn't even have considered leaving early. That would have been rude.

Once, at the Mt. Olive Missionary Baptist Church in Muskegon Heights, at a service filled with deep, haunting music that transported me to another world, the minister, Pastor Walter Butts, commented on this with some surprise.

"So many politicians come here, speak, and then leave," he told the congregation. "But we are at the end of our service and Mary Valentine is still here." After that, I heard I developed a reputation – the politician who stayed until the end of the service.

At another church service, the minister announced to the congregation that God had told him someone was there that day who needed extra prayers.

"Mary Valentine, will you please come up?" he requested.

He was absolutely right. I needed extra prayers that day— I was exhausted from all the door knocking and fund-raising. I then participated in what is called a laying-on of hands. First, the minister called me to the front of the congregation, then several women from the congregation stood behind me, murmuring random words. I believe this is called speaking in tongues. It was a beautiful experience, and I felt great reverence for all those who came up to the front of the church to pray over me.

I loved knocking on doors in the African-American community. The people I met on doorsteps, porches, and in apartment buildings were invariably warm, friendly, and encouraging. I always felt safe and welcome. The idea that we white people need to be afraid to walk into an African-American community is racist nonsense.

The Highs: Volunteers, New Friends, and Parades!

I had so many wonderful volunteers and staffers when I ran for state Senate—as I had in my other campaigns. I met quite a few Democrats in Newaygo County who had been volunteering for local elections year after year in the face of incredibly bad odds—the county is so strongly Republican, I think the county line is painted red. Yet these brave souls never give up. And I met people in Ludington who were as unique as the town itself. Ludington is the only town I know of that has a mural committee. Yes, that's right, a mural committee. They have worked to create murals around the town relating the city's history: a delightful touch for tourists and exciting for Senate candidates who appreciate public art.

I also need to mention Calder Bergam from Muskegon, a bright, hard-working young man and a long-time family friend. And I'm grateful to Branden Gemzer, former candidate for the 91st District, which I was vacating. Branden offered his vast skills to our campaign, and Cyndy Viars worked tirelessly for a time as well. Tim Hanson was on board working the northern counties, along with my daughter Robin.

In fact, hundreds of people volunteered—too many to name. Each of these volunteers was dear to me then, and is dear to me now. People constantly were showing up to knock on doors, make phone calls, enter data, walk in parades, hand out literature, host house parties, bring in food, put up and take down signs, and more—the list of jobs is endless. I'm deeply grateful to the volunteers for their love and support.

And then there were the parades! Some of my sweetest political memories are of parades in small towns: The Asparagus Parade in Oceana County, the Old Fashioned Days Parade in Fruitport, the National Baby Food Festival Parade in Fremont, parades in Ludington, Holton, Roosevelt Park—and even the Croton Hardy Dam.

In the northern counties, Dallas Dean, long-time Democrat, brought his van, which pulled a small flatbed wagon with white railings. Before the parade started, volunteers pitched in, putting up signs of local politicians on the railings, along with banners and flags to make it festive. Dallas always played good old patriotic music, which blasted out of the large speakers on his van.

Before every parade, our team put out the call for volunteers to walk with us. We usually had five to ten loyal volunteers who put on good walking shoes and our blue Mary Valentine tee shirts. They walked with me along the parade route, handing out candy and lapel stickers to spectators. When Dallas' small van was not available, we slapped some Mary Valentine posters on a car, which drove along with us as well. And of course, Chris Kilgroe was there at nearly every single parade—organizing parade walkers, making sure everyone had a tee shirt, and handing out stickers and candy.

The Croton-Hardy Dam parade couldn't be surpassed for pure fun. It's likely not one 34th District Democratic voter was there, but people were waving from boats, laughing, and having a blast. Joviality was everywhere.

I was a little afraid to participate in the National Baby Food Parade in Fremont, a strongly Republican small town in Newaygo County, north of Muskegon. For decades, the Democratic message there has been so badly twisted by our Republican friends that I'm quite certain they think we Democrats have a plan to kill babies in our spare time and make sure every last citizen is on welfare. So I was afraid that parade-goers would boo me—and my companions—when we walked along Main Street. I braced myself for a rough parade route, but it was unnecessary. The people of Fremont love their parade, and gave us a warm reception. This was in part because my parents, Bob and Phyl Hostetler, had been owners of Fremont's weekly newspaper—the *Fremont Times-Indicator*—for several years. My brother, Doug, and his wife,

Judy, owned it for a while as well. Many of their friends came to the parade that July day and yelled encouragement to us. In the end, it was a great day and we had a lovely time.

One of the highlights of many of the parades we walked in was the brainchild of Norma York-Bremer and her family. After the first parade, Norma, her daughter, Kirsten, and her sweet granddaughters, Caitlin and Bronwyn, realized there were far too many hungry, thirsty dogs in the crowd. So the York-Bremer family put together little packets of dog biscuits and small bottles of water, and covered the packets with Mary Valentine stickers. At every parade Caitlyn and Bronwyn sought out dogs of all types and supplied them with food and water from a wagon decorated with flags and tributes to those serving in the Armed Forces. This final touch was courtesy of their mom, Kirsten.

This brings me to a little story about how utterly ridiculous politics have become across our land in recent years.

When a Republican operative noticed that the brand of water Caitlin and Bronwyn were handing out was Ice Mountain, he wrote a nasty letter to the editor about how awful I was for using Ice Mountain water (which is the water Nestle pulls from the ground in northern Michigan). Apparently, he was offended that the York-Bremer family would use this water, despite the fact that preserving our groundwater is something I fully support. I was just so happy to have young people doing this, I didn't even notice the brand name of the water—and probably wouldn't have said anything even if I had. Thankfully, Norma replied to that letter with a pithy letter of her own, telling him to leave her grandchildren alone.

Another high point of my senate run was being able to stay at the home of Chrissy Hall, a Ludington Democrat. I took a few members of my staff and traveled to Ludington for several days at a time to knock on doors in Mason County, which is where Ludington is located. After we did some concentrated canvassing, my poll numbers in that area improved. Chrissy offered us her guest home, which was big enough for my daughter Robin, staffer Tim Hansen, and myself to each have our own room. Mine overlooked a small orchard, where one morning I saw two fawns frolicking in the grass. It was wonderful to stay there, but we worked hard, too—canvassing day and night.

That senate campaign was such a concerted effort. We never slowed down and never gave up—even after poor poll results or the loss of key endorsements. There was still so much positive energy and support, and we always felt heartened after we had knocked on some doors—people were so encouraging. For a long time, it seemed winning was possible. But the truth is, my opposition spent three or possibly even four times more money than I was able to spend, much of it bashing me, which is pretty much impossible to overcome. As my campaign drew closer to the actual Election Day, my staff and I felt caught in a downward spiral.

The Low Points: A Legal Nightmare, a Lost Endorsement, and a Dirty Campaign

We had large signs that said "Re-Elect Mary Valentine for State Representative" from the previous campaign. Being good stewards of our resources, we decided to recycle them. One team of volunteers covered up the "Re-Elect" sticker with one that said "Elect." Another team covered the "State Representative" with a sticker that said "State Senator." And yet another team put the signs up all over town. Unknown to headquarters, one of the signs somehow fell through the crack and went up saying "Re-Elect Mary Valentine for State

Senator." One sign. So the guy who is now our state senator sued me. I'm not kidding—he sued.

Shortly after the signs went up, in early October, I received a call at our headquarters from Geoff Hansen's lawyer stating the sign needed to be taken down immediately and that I was about to be sued. Within ten minutes, the offending sign was repaired and all other signs were double-checked. That didn't stop Goeff Hansen, though—he moved forward with his suit against me. Later, as I recall, he claimed this was done behind his back, and he had had no knowledge of it. His name was right there on the papers that were served, though. He was definitely the one suing me.

Yup. I was hauled into court for making a small mistake. Eric Gaertner, *Chronicle* reporter, was there as well, with a *Chronicle* photographer. Although this had been an oversight and had been corrected immediately after we became aware of it, the judge, The Honorable John C. Ruck, made a big show of lecturing me before he would dismiss the case. He was infuriatingly condescending in his lecture, and I'm certain it was done to win points with his Republican buddies. In my view, he should have been lecturing Hansen (who, by the way, didn't even have the guts to show up) for wasting the court's time with this political stunt. The reporter and photographer from the *Chronicle* were there from start to finish, making no effort to hide their silly grins at my come-uppance. The whole thing lasted about ten minutes. It was not only humiliating, it was pointless and costly for taxpayers.

And though the *Muskegon Chronicle* never managed to find the time or space to print any of the news releases sent out by staff about important legislation, this story was spread across the front page of the paper the next day, with photos to boot.

The *Ludington Daily News* (LDN) also covered the story and wrote an editorial about it in the Friday, October 8, edition. They agreed with me that the lawsuit was a step too far, and a waste of taxpayer time and money. They even pointed out that it harmed the image of both candidates, and elected officials in general. I couldn't agree more. They also commented that this seemed out of character for Hansen and perhaps he was talked into it, letting him off the hook. What? Since when is it okay to let others convince you to do something wrong? Don't we desperately need people of integrity and honor to serve in the legislature—people who know right from wrong and are willing to do the right thing, even when it is difficult? Allowing someone to talk you into something is not an example of courage and integrity—it's an example of weakness. Apparently, his nice-guy image hides the lack of character that would allow him to go along with this.

Another devastating low in my campaign came when the Black Women's Political Caucus of Muskegon endorsed Goeff Hansen. As the African-American community is largely Democratic, that endorsement was an arrow through my heart. The *Chronicle*, the same paper that rarely bothered to cover any story about policy being promoted in Lansing, made a big deal of this endorsement. I am happy to report, though, that in spite of that endorsement, the vote totals from Muskegon Heights were strongly in my favor.

Before Election Day, voters received numerous fliers about me from my opponent's campaign. I wasn't keeping count, but Chris Kilgroe, a stickler for facts, said it was eighteen in all. Nearly every piece of literature repeated the same one-word slip-of-the-tongue I had made during the last campaign—that I voted *for* taxes as often as I could, when I had meant to say I voted *against* taxes as often as I could (referring to my first term in office, before the global financial debacle of 2008). Although it was clear from the context of my speech that I had intended to say *against*, not *for* tax increases (not to mention my voting record), the misstated remark showed up on nearly every piece of literature Goeff Hansen's team sent out in their efforts to discredit me.

As I mentioned earlier, Hansen also had accused me publicly of wanting to put everyone's water under the complete control of the state. This accusation carried not one iota of truth, but he didn't let that stop him. He repeated it on a TV ad that played over and over again. I considered suing him, but research taught me that in Michigan, a political candidate is allowed to make such statements. What a shame for voters, as they try to figure out who can best represent their interests.

Hansen put out one particularly insulting TV ad with my face on a cereal box. What was the fictitious name of this cereal? Tax Cereal, of course. Hansen even wore a grocer's apron in the ad, pretending to be a grocer himself, and the cereal box had a long and ridiculous list of taxes on it, which I supposedly wanted to impose on people because I love taxes so much.

What is my real record on the issue of taxes? Where do I begin?

When I first began my service for the state, Michigan still had good schools, with low class sizes, professional librarians, and appropriate services for Special Education students. We also still had an adequate number of public safety officers working on our behalf. We had resources to keep murderers locked up in prisons where they belonged. But between Republican tax cuts, the demise of manufacturing, and the global economic crash, our revenues had been gutted. We Democrats were continually trying to figure out how we could keep Michigan's tradition of high-quality public service and public safety. The Republicans, on the other hand, were dedicated entirely to assuring that not one extra dime in new revenues would come into our state coffers.

As a result of all of this, during my second term, the Democratic House offered several bills to increase revenues for the purpose of keeping adequate public services and public safety intact, which the Republican Senate always voted down. I believe in high-quality public services. I believe they make our state more attractive for those wanting to come to our state and for those who live here. So I voted for those revenues. None of them ever passed, but trying to get *something* passed during my second term, I racked up a voting record that was easily twisted. Although overwhelmingly, no one ever paid a dime for any of those taxes I voted on, that fact, strangely, never made it into the ads put out by the Hansen campaign.

Interestingly, when the Republicans voted to bring in revenues, they called them revenue enhancements. When we Democrats did the same thing, they called them huge tax increases. Even more interesting, after the election of 2010, when Republicans were in charge of the entire government, they voted in tax increases all over the place—not on the wealthy, mind you, but on the most vulnerable. It's not surprising that they raised taxes—Michigan simply didn't have enough revenues to function adequately. The surprising thing was that, not only did they significantly raise taxes, they slashed funding for public services. They were clever about it, though—promising never to raise taxes, then only raising them on those least able to pay.

The other tax I'd like to explain is related to the mountains of out-of-state trash coming into our state from all over the country, even from as far away as Florida. Companies send their trash here, tearing up our roads and bridges and contaminating our water supply, for one reason and one reason alone. Michigan is cheap. And because of interstate commerce laws, we can't charge more for out-of-state trash than for that generated within our own state. We charge 21 cents a ton—as opposed to states like Pennsylvania, which had a similar problem and increased its charge to $7.50 a ton. The tax increase amounts to something like a dollar a month for most citizens. I ran on the issue of stopping out-of-state trash, so of course I voted for that tax increase, which is what the people want. This was one of the taxes mentioned in the "tax cereal" ad. Had it passed, it would have been insignificant to citizens. But since that bill never made it through the Michigan Senate, not one citizen ever paid a dime for that tax. The same is true for most of the other tax increases mentioned in the Hansen campaign's anti-Valentine literature.

Throughout the entire election cycle, polls across the state—and the entire country—predicted that the elections of 2010 would produce big wins for the Republican Party. "You have nothing to lose at this point, Mary," Mark Fisk told me. "Call Hansen out on his negative ads."

So I did. It took guts on my part, and I'm still not sure if it was the right thing to do, but I called him out on the negativity of his campaign at every turn. I exposed the phony lawsuit, the insulting literature pieces, and the TV ads with their false assertions that I wanted to put peoples' water under complete state control. In the end, my objections did no good, but they had an unexpected result. In the course of stating the truth boldly, I shed my "good girl" persona and spoke out with strength and conviction on issues I care about, even the most controversial ones.

One more thing happened during the campaign that caused some confusion for Goeff Hansen's family. And from what I hear, they've not been shy about criticizing me for it. When the issue of water—and the questions it generated—went on and on, a decision was made to issue a robotic (robo) call to citizens of the district trying to clarify the issue. At that point, groups in Michigan attempting to discredit me had produced many ads that directed citizens to contact our office. My staff had important work to do—helping constituents, researching legislation, and managing committee work. But every time a new ad came out, they were inundated with calls from constituents and had to spend a good deal of time clarifying the misinformation the ads put out.

Putting the legislative phone number on those ads lacked integrity in my view. We don't need taxpayer-funded staff fielding calls from political ads or issue ads. So those who prepared our robo call sought out Hansen's political number, which was listed on the paperwork registered with the state. Turned out Hansen had put his home phone number on that paper work, rather than a number at his campaign headquarters. Although we didn't use that phone number in anger or to harm Hansen's family, before long, they were facing the same kind of calls my staff had been fielding for weeks. We heard bitter complaints from his family about how evil I was to put his phone number on that robo call. I heard one of those complaints again just last week.

One More Low Point

I hoped in vain that the *Muskegon Chronicle* would consider my hard work and four years of service when they chose which candidate to endorse. No such luck. I was hopeful in part because in the months before their endorsement of Hansen, the *Chronicle* had featured a long series about the importance of education. I knew Senator Hansen and his party had no commitment to adequately funding education. But that apparently wasn't an important consideration for the paper's endorsement.[25]

I have some small comfort in knowing that, in the end, I could have done nothing to change that election's outcome. The way I understand it, Democrats stayed away from the polls in droves while Republicans turned out. Independents voted Republican. Democrats lost across the state and the country—excellent lawmakers and leaders left public office. And the citizens have paid a steep price for the policies that have been put in place as a result, with lower paying jobs, inferior education, fewer safeguards for clean air and water, and an increase in the income inequality that plagues our country.

The State of Our State

The results of the 2010 election, I'm sad to report, have further devastated Michigan. Instead of strengthening laws to protect our air and water, the Republican legislature weakened those laws. We now have small-time dictators, called Emergency Managers, in charge of our most vulnerable cities and school districts, and these unelected dictators can—and do—ignore the concerns of local citizens. The people voted to repeal the Emergency Manager Law, but the Republican legislature ignored the people, voting it right back into law. The legislature's fear of having citizens stand up for their own

---

[25] It turned out I was right by the way—school funding has been cut so dramatically since Republicans took office that schools across our state are in bankruptcy. Class sizes are rising. Social workers have been let go. School nurses and trained librarians are largely a thing of the past. Our young people are paying the price for this lack of concern for education.

rights and interests inspired them to add appropriations into several extremely controversial bills. As a result of those small appropriations, those bills, when passed into law, cannot be repealed by citizen groups, something our constitution allows for.

And here is another great irony: Senator Goeff Hansen, who falsely accused me of wanting to put people's water under the complete control of the state, supported the bill to put Emergency Managers in charge of some of our school districts and communities. As a result, many communities and school districts across our state are under the complete control of the state with no local control whatsoever.

All of this has been very bad for Michigan's residents.

One Final High Note and Thank You – The Greenville Example

A highlight of my Senate campaign was when Jennifer Granholm attended one of my fundraisers, at the home of Tyler and Susan Newton, high on a bluff overlooking Lake Michigan. It was a hot summer day; our entire staff attended the event, and, although Granholm's popularity was low, we were all thrilled to meet her personally. During her speech, she shared insight into what she described as a pivotal event of her years in the governorship. She talked about a company that produces home appliances of all sorts, Electrolux, which had been located in Greenville, a small town in mid-Michigan. For decades, Electrolux had been the heart and soul of Greenville, employing many of the residents there. Shortly after Governor Granholm was first elected, Electrolux made the decision to move its operations to Mexico. Governor Granholm then described to us her efforts to keep Electrolux in Greenville. She offered the company every tax break, every

Mary Valentine

tax rebate, anything she could think of to convince them to stay in Michigan. The company officials were unswayed. "There is absolutely nothing you can do that would tempt us to stay," they told the governor. "We are leaving Michigan and nothing you can offer us will change that." Electrolux left in September 2006. Greenville's economy collapsed. This happened in a decade during which the manufacturing industry in Michigan was destroyed, the loss bringing with it all of the accompanying problems that come with the loss of jobs. Time and again that same scenario played out, for manufacturers all over the state. Many other companies told their governor: "There is nothing you can do to change our mind about leaving Michigan."

More recently, thanks to the bailout of the auto industry, Michigan is recovering and good-paying jobs are returning. Although some spoke out against the auto bailout as being too expensive, the auto industry has since repaid all the money they borrowed. But in those dark days of the 2000s, Michigan was caught in an out-of-control downward spiral. Jobs disappeared by droves in cities large and small. Governor Granholm's strategy was to follow the lead of more prosperous states by increasing the number of college-educated people and diversifying the economy. I agreed with this approach to the state's economic problems.

When I lived in the Upper Peninsula's Iron Mountain in the early 1970s, I learned a little about the history of that region. Twice, the town of Iron Mountain was devastated by the loss of an industry. First, the mining industry left, destroying the town financially. Then the Ford Company came to the region and built factories to supply parts for the wooden-paneled Model A car, also called the Tin Lizzie or Flivver, which was produced by the Ford Company from 1908 to 1927. Ford located in Kingsford, Iron Mountain's twin city,

and stayed until the late 1950s, when Ford pulled its factories out of the region. The economy of Dickinson County,
where Iron Mountain is located, crashed once again. The city
leaders took stock and decided it was time to diversify their
economy. They built an industrial park and recruited small
factories to locate there. Since then, the town has hummed
along. Diversification was a winning strategy for Iron Mountain in the 1950s—and could be a winning strategy for
Michigan today.

When Governor Granholm first took office, back in 2003,
she took a rather traditional path for governors in her situation—she cut taxes, hoping the cuts would reinvigorate the
economy. This approach wasn't successful, in part because
Michigan's economic problems didn't arise out of a flawed tax
policy, but grew out of our total dependence on the auto
industry. When it collapsed, we were lost.

It's clear: We need to analyze the challenges Michigan
faces, identify solutions based on that analysis, and then
implement the changes. If the problem with the economy is
the result of our tax policy, change the policy. If it's an over-
reliance on one industry, bring greater business diversity into
the state. If it's a dearth of educated citizens, make an
investment in educating Michigan's children and adults. But
if the economy needs diversifying and the population needs
educating, cutting taxes alone simply won't solve the problem.

When Governor Granholm and her staff studied the au-
tomobile industry, they realized that electric cars were the
wave of the future. She and President Obama created tax
incentive packages intended to bring battery companies to
Michigan, thus creating a whole new industry. I have great
respect and admiration for Jennifer Granholm—I'm grateful
for her efforts to diversify the economy and promote educa-

tion while serving as governor. She helped us through a uniquely difficult era in our state history.

I'm sorry to report that much of her work was undone when the Republicans took charge: the fall of the film industry and the demise of the Michigan Promise, to name two. Happily, her work to further fund preschool education has continued past her tenure. Thanks to her efforts, Michigan's preschool programs, though still in need of expansion, are one of the bright spots in our education landscape. Clean air and water received strong protection under her watch as well.

Chapter XXI

FAQ

"Are you THE Mary Valentine?" asks the young man at the Sherwin-Williams paint store, as he stirs the paint I'm purchasing for my bathroom ceiling. When I tell him I am indeed, he says, "I remember you from sobriety court. That was a good program and it helped me a lot."

Moments like this pleasantly surprise me and are the up side of having put myself in the public arena—win or lose. I often feel the glow of being remembered for something I stood up for, or some way I helped a family or individual in trouble. It's part of my identity now, and I like that.

* * * *

In 2005, when I first decided to try to get myself elected, I was unknown to the general public. My husband and I moved to Norton Shores from Grand Rapids in 1988 and raised our family here. I knew many people in my own private life: our neighbors, my children's friends and teachers, and other couples, colleagues, and friends from our tiny church, Unity of Muskegon. Yet I had no public persona. Eight years later, after thousands of doors knocked and hundreds of thousands of dollars in advertisements, along with four years of being on radio, TV, and in the newspaper, I no longer live a life of quiet anonymity.

Initially, when people recognized me as Mary Valentine, the former state representative, I felt an odd combination of embarrassment and joy. I didn't know exactly what to say or do. I'm sure I appeared as a deer in the headlights to many. Now I smile, shake hands, introduce myself, and inquire about the person who has approached me, enjoying the moment. I occasionally get comments when I'm buying something at the grocery store or standing in line at a restaurant. My favorite incident, though, was when I was having a burger and a Corona with some friends at Tipsy Toad in downtown Muskegon. A white, middle-aged woman walked over and looked straight at me.

"Did anyone ever tell you that you're the spitting image of Mary Valentine?" she asked.

"Well, that's because I *am* Mary Valentine," said I, followed by a great deal of laughter from all.

Once, when I was selecting a cell phone at the Verizon Store, the young man waiting on me gave no indication that he knew who I was. But at the end of the transaction, he commented that his grandma was a real fan of mine.

"Where does she live?" I asked.

When I learned she lived only a few blocks away from my house, I dropped in to see her on my way home. Needless to say, she was a bit shocked to see me at her door. I told her I had just met her grandson and he wanted me to say hello.

Many lovely perks come with being a public person.

Other moments, though, leave me shaking my head in frustration—such as when someone approaches me to continue an old argument, adamant that they know my stand on this or that issue—even though I have no idea who they are and where they got their information. Even so, when this happens I stand my ground, look the person straight in the eye, and tell them what I really think.

"That's not what you believe," one man said, after approaching me and bringing up the water tax issue.

I wanted to say: *Really? Really?? You've never talked with me, but you know me better than I know myself?*" I held my tongue, though, smiled politely, and went on my way.

Mostly, however, I welcome the questions that come from having been in the public eye. Here are some I am asked most frequently.

Did working as a state representative in Lansing live up to your expectations?

The truth is I had no idea what to expect, so I wasn't disappointed. Nor was it better than I expected. I just took my new role as it came, tried to be true to myself, and served my constituents—both personally and politically.

There sure were some surprises along the way, though!

One big surprise was that the life of a legislator is so completely unpredictable. A legislative session could last from one full hour, to one full day, to one full week. You never knew for sure how long you were in for. Sometimes, you could sense that a long session was coming, but you never could be certain. Often, I'd come to a session expecting to be there all day, and leave after a few hours. Other times, I'd expect to be in session a few hours, and be there for 24 hours. Soon after I figured this out, I brought a small pillow from home and kept it on a ledge beneath my desk. When leadership was discussing an issue late into the night and I found myself dozing off in my chair, I'd head into the caucus room for a catnap. Once I made the mistake of nodding off in my chair at 3:00 a.m.

"Be careful," a colleague warned, "someone could take your picture and use it against you."

Such is life in the days of stiff partisanship.

Frankly, I never failed to be surprised when I looked around the chamber at 3:00 a.m. to see everything going on as it had been for hour upon hour—clerks clerking, lobbyists hanging out in the lobby, legislators at their desk answering e-mails, and policy people running back and forth drafting bills and amendments. The news media were at their stations, watching our every move. Everybody just continued working as though nothing was unusual about a fully functioning legislature in the wee hours of the morning.

Then, suddenly, the gavel would pound and the speaker pro-tem would holler: "There will be no more voting and the members are free to leave."

Once we were dismissed at 6:00 a.m., right in the middle of a ferocious blizzard. I wanted to get home so badly, I checked out of my room at the Radisson and started the trip back to Norton Shores, even though the roads were a slippery mess and I was exhausted. The blizzard cost me a full hour of driving just to get across Lansing, so I checked into a Residence Inn near M-96 and slept for several hours, until I was awake enough to try again. Luckily the snow had stopped, and I finally drove home.

Such is the life of a state representative in the snow belt of Michigan.

How could you stand the constant, intense partisanship?

The truth is, legislators tend to be a congenial group of people who can get along fine in day-to-day transactions. We didn't necessarily like each other's votes or stands on various issues, but we were glad to congratulate each other on new marriages and new grandchildren. We sympathized with deaths and illnesses. We wished each other happy birthday, Merry Christmas, and Happy New Year. We often showed concern for one another at the end of a night session, when many of us began our long journeys across the state to our home districts.

"Drive carefully," we said to one another as we left the building.

At the same time, though, we tried to defeat one another, both at the polls and with contentious legislation. This made for an odd juxtaposition—friend and foe at the same time— unlike any previous job I had ever had.

Another surprise: Everyone in Lansing treats the state representatives like royalty. I didn't mind, of course, but it was a bit of a shock—and at times, aggravating. If I reached the elevator at the same time as another person and he or she walked in before me, they apologized profusely. "Non-sense," I would insist. "We are all people here, no one is above another."

I was equally surprised by how some people really resented our salaries. It was a hard job, darn it—demanding and endlessly stressful. Imagine trying to please 90,000 people at the same time! Cutting the pay of legislators is not a solution to any of our problems; it's simply a red herring. We should all stop complaining about legislators' salaries—most of them earn their pay and more. I also stood up for government workers of all types getting good pay and benefits.

What are your thoughts about Emergency Managers?

In my opinion, less extreme steps should be taken first when a district nears bankruptcy. For one thing, we should more adequately fund our cities and school districts so they don't so easily approach bankruptcy. But if municipalities or school districts truly are overspending, one option might be for the state to require periodic performance audits they must pass to gain additional funding. If the state legislature only could drop the ideological warfare and put their heads together, I'm sure they could come up with less radical solutions that would help foundering districts while still preserving democracy.

Do "back room" politics still exist in Lansing?

Back-room politics are an important part of the process of governing in a democracy. A positive example of this occurred during my second term, when I chaired the Family and Children's Services Committee. We were working on legislation that would improve care to children by requiring better training for childcare providers. Apparently, several stakeholders had been arguing about the details for quite some time, and many thought having another conversation about it was useless. As chair, it was my call to facilitate that conversation. At my suggestion, we pulled our chairs up to the oval table on the 11th floor conference room in the House Office Building. I dusted off my long-buried skills as a marriage counselor (one of my job duties when I was a social worker at Child and Family Services in Marquette back in the late 1970s), and gave each person an opportunity to state his or case regarding this issue. After everyone moved an inch or two closer to a solution, people made compromises they might not otherwise have thought possible. In the end, everyone left that meeting with a smile on his or her face, and we were able to bring the bill up for discussion in committee. That, in my opinion, is an example of how back-room politics should work: Give lawmakers a forum and the opportunity to compromise.

The process is far smoother when lawmakers and stakeholders can speak freely and no one from the press is there—ready to take things out of context to create a controversy. In the end, I believe transparency is important, but sometimes the process of hammering out details can be more efficient and effective if it is done out of range of TV cameras.

Of course, there is a dark side to the back-room politics model. It leaves legislators more vulnerable to threats—stated or unstated. Hidden from the public eye, leadership might well punish legislators who won't go along with them, taking away committee assignments or chairmanships. Blessedly, I never had to face such threats myself. The closest I came, which was really no fun and involved no threats—was during the tax wars of 2007, mentioned earlier in this book.

But such is the life of the back-room lawmakers, trying to pass a few good laws that would make life easier for the people of Michigan.

Two questions I frequently asked myself while in office were:

How does allowing rights for one family ruin another family, as pro-family legislators claim?

If my sister Maggie Hostetler and her lifelong partner since 1981, Lorri Sipes, were allowed to get married in Michigan, how in the world would that hurt my family or anybody else's? Being denied the same legal rights as heterosexual couples can, in some circumstance, devastate a loving family, particularly if children are involved.

How does criminalizing the ability of a scared 12-year-old to get an abortion make a family stronger?

The answer is that it doesn't. If the worst happens and a 12-year-old becomes pregnant, I simply don't believe a distant lawmaker should make the decision about whether that child will be forced to continue the pregnancy. I think the decision should be in the hands of those who know that child.

I still believe that what helps families thrive is having the right to earn a decent living, be safe on the job, have a roof over their heads, and get a good education. Families need access to quality healthcare and clean air. These are what build strong families. Yet these are the exactly what the pro-family Republicans oppose.

I'm afraid this will never stop amazing me. Nor will it ever stop astounding me that so many people buy this nonsense.

Chapter XXII

Still More Questions

The 2012 election is over. Obama won, and many of us heaved a deep sigh of relief. The Republican propaganda machine was working so furiously in the weeks before the election that they believed their own nonsense. They couldn't imagine that our country would re-elect Barack Obama. As a result, even with many projections of an Obama victory staring them in the face, the GOP couldn't believe Romney would lose. Even after the fact, they couldn't believe that he had lost. But Obama won decisively, and it's my fervent hope that the Republican Party does at least two things in coming elections. First, I hope that party leaders will double-check their facts and stick to them in all talking points, rather than pretending reality doesn't exist. Second, I hope the GOP realizes that if they remain a party consisting mainly of white men, they'll never win the presidency again.

In the 21st century, inclusion, honesty, and meeting the needs of all the people are the winning ticket.

Collene Lamonte, Democratic Candidate in the 91st District, won in a squeaker and put my old seat back into Democratic hands. That was a great source of joy and relief for me—like a full circle had been completed.

On a personal note, I woke up one morning recently without anger. My anger toward the media and Goeff Hansen, as well as my personal anger toward the Republican Party, had evaporated. I still want them to become good citizens of this country—and to work for the people who live here. And I still intend to speak out when I feel it is necessary. But my personal anger related to the campaign has dissipated—at least for the moment.

Although I am still frustrated, it is now less personal and more about the legislative work that is harming our state. There are days when I think my life would be much easier if I didn't know what I do about the decisions being made in Lansing.

Anger is a natural part of losing such a huge campaign. Everyone goes through it. I am just glad to be largely on the other side of it. Having moved through that anger has allowed me to concentrate more fully on doing my part to shape a future in which the middle class can flourish, our next generation can receive a top-notch education, all of our citizens can thrive, and equality really will prevail.

The struggle continues. I hope you will join it.

* * * *

Where Did the Middle Class Go?

When I was a kid, my dad, a history major, journalist, and generally thoughtful guy, told me, "The reason we have a democracy is because we have a strong middle class." He was right. And I'm deeply troubled by the fact that the middle class in America is steadily shrinking, while the number of individuals and families living in poverty has increased in our great country. Iray Nabatoff, Louisiana citizen and chair of United Nonprofits of Greater New Orleans, put it more succinctly (when quoted in an article in *The Nation*): "Poverty is creeping into the diminished middle class."[26]

And as we lose the strength that comes from a solid middle class, citizens lose faith in their government, become discouraged, and stop participating. This gives the wealthy and power-hungry an ever-increasing say in public policies intended to award them more wealth and power. Those policies rob the working classes of their hope of prosperity. In turn, working people become less engaged politically, handing even more power over to those who already have an overabundance of wealth and power. This vicious downward cycle leads to a shrinking middle class and expanding poverty. Without a middle class, democracy contracts—just like my wise father said.

Consider the recent voter suppression laws, the gerrymandering of congressional districts, and the January 21, 2010, Supreme Court ruling that corporations are people and can give unlimited funds anonymously to political candidates. All these actions result in a democracy in jeopardy.

Where Did Civil Discourse Go?

In 1987, the FCC repealed the Fairness Doctrine, which led directly to extreme-right radio personalities, such as Rush Limbaugh (who has been on the radio with "The Rush Limbaugh Show" since 1988), becoming increasingly outrageous—fanning the flames of polarization with lies and name-calling. The Sandra Fluke affair is but one example. When this young woman testified that health insurance should

[26] Sasha Abromsky, "The Other America, 2012: Confronting the Poverty Epidemic," *The Nation*, April 25, 2012.

cover birth control pills and that women often use them for medical reasons other than birth control, Limbaugh blasted her on the airwaves, calling her a slut. He said that she was having so much sex that she could hardly walk. He said that if she was asking the government to pay for her birth control, she should make sex tapes available for all by airing them publicly.

Unbelievable.

Even more unbelievable to me is that I heard people repeating that line of thought when I was knocking on doors for a political candidate. Clearly, some people aren't ignoring Rush. Instead, they're using him as a role model. Limbaugh's vitriolic treatment of Sandra Fluke—his misinformation and name-calling—has no place in the public discourse. I can't understand why no one in the Republican Party ever holds this man accountable for his behavior.

When I bring up the issue of civility with conservatives, instead of condemning Limbaugh's latest diatribe, they point to Rachel Maddow and claim that liberal Democrats do the same thing. And while it's true that Maddow has a liberal perspective, there is no valid comparison. Her facts are meticulously researched, and reported without name-calling and disrespect. In all the years that "The Rachel Maddow Show" has been on MSNBC, I've never seen her be hateful and combative in her commentary. I have seen times when her commentary was slanted, but it has always seemed accurate and respectful. Comparing her show with Limbaugh's is a false equivalency. The only thing these two commentators have in common is that they both have a clear point of view. My friends on the other side of the aisle refuse to own up to who and what Rush Limbaugh is, and the damage he has done to civility in political discourse.

Our country has faced unbelievable challenges in the past: the Civil War, slavery, the Great Depression and two World Wars. We put a stop to the corruption of the Gilded Age and put laws in place to protect working Americans from unsafe working conditions. We saved rivers, lakes, and streams by adopting policies to protect them from the polluters. But to overcome hardship and protect our citizens, we've always had to face our problems head-on—both parties working together to find reasonable solutions.

In our current political climate, denial, misinformation, dismissive attitudes, and false equivalencies are the closest we get to reasonable dialogue. Often these strategies mask dire problems that desperately need solutions. Name-calling and misrepresentation succeed in shaming decent people into silence. Every time another person is silenced, our democracy is weaker, and effective solutions are further delayed.

Another symptom of our current lack of honesty in politics: bizarre definitions of what it means to be a Democrat. I've heard Democratic voters called "lazy liberals," "union thugs," even "baby killers." Conservatives and Republicans tell our citizens that Democrats want to take people's hard-earned money away from them and give it to lazy poor people—that they don't want people to earn their own money. That's simply not true. They don't even call us Democrats— they call us "tax-and-spend Democrats." None of these characterizations of Democrats is true, but Republicans and right-wing think tanks, like the Mackinac Center, continuously push these ideas to frighten people out of voting for leaders who have their best interests at heart. Ironically, many of the people hurt most by Republican policy are unwilling to consider voting for a Democrat, even as democracy is pulled right out from under them.

President Barack Obama often has said that, as a nation, we should assure that all citizens have opportunity. He pointed out that he and Michelle weren't born with silver spoons in their mouths, but that they were provided opportunities along the way that enabled them to use their God-given talents. This way of defining progress is something with which most Americans agree. Mitt Romney, in his failed run for the presidency in 2012, managed to twist Obama's statements about opportunity. He claimed that President Obama was attacking Romney's own wealthy background. His supporters believed him, and accused Obama of making a vicious personal attack on the wealth of the Romney family.

This is but another example of false equivalencies taking the place of a real discussion in our current political landscape.

Where Did Fair Wages Go?

Shortly after the 2010 election, when Republicans made a clean sweep across the nation—particularly in Michigan, where they now have complete control of all branches of state government—I read the transcript of a speech that Bill Moyers gave in 2010 as part of the Howard Zinn Lecture Series at Boston University, titled "Welcome to the Plutocracy." This speech, which has been widely shared via the Internet, should be required reading for all Americans. Moyers outlines what is happening to our country, discussing a phenomenon called "wage repression," and stressing that we are losing ground as a great nation because of it:

> "Wage repression," [has] been happening in
> our country since around 1980. I must invoke
> some statistics here, knowing that statistics

can glaze the eyes; but if indeed it's the mark of a truly educated person to be deeply moved by statistics, as I once read, surely this truly educated audience will be moved by the recent analysis of tax data by the economists Thomas Piketty and Emmanuel Saez. They found that from 1950 through 1980, the share of all income in America going to everyone but the rich increased from 64 percent to 65 percent. Because the nation's economy was growing handsomely, the average income for 9 out of 10 Americans was growing, too – from $17,719 to $30,941. That's a 75 percent increase in income in constant 2008 dollars.

But then it stopped. Since 1980 the economy has also continued to grow handsomely, but only a fraction at the top have benefitted. The line flattens for the bottom 90% of Americans. Average income went from that $30,941 in 1980 to $31,244 in 2008. Think about that: the average income of Americans increased just $303 dollars in 28 years.

That's wage repression.

And how is it that the wealthiest among us have hoodwinked everyday Americans into believing this isn't so, even as we live it and experience the effects every single day? How do they convince the average citizen that what is happening is good for our country? They do it with spin, misinformation, denial, false equivalencies, and the constant discrediting of anyone who disagrees. How, I wonder, will we ever be able to make solid decisions based on misinformation? How long can we keep denying what we see happening before our very eyes?

Where Did Our Public Education System Go?

The plan to eliminate public entities has been carefully laid out for decades, and is now being implemented in Michigan, as well as in other states. One example of that: the public schools. If we don't change direction, within a few years most, if not all, of our schools will be for profit.

"That's good," some say, "because competition will make our schools strong."

The truth is that competition creates winners and losers. This strategy might possibly create some good, for-profit schools—well-funded "Cadillac" schools. But for every good, for-profit school, there will be many more jalopies—for-profits that spend our tax money on spin and public relations (not to mention their own financial gain), while they cheat students out of art and music classes. The students who need the most services and advantages from these schools will be the least likely to receive them.

Funding for public education has dropped dramatically. Charter schools (publicly funded but usually run by for-profit operators) are proliferating. Untested, for-profit cyber-schools are increasing. Meanwhile, funding for traditional neighborhood schools—with solid music, athletic, art, and academic programs as well as special education programs—has been cut dramatically.

Our public schools are in deep trouble. But sadly, few superintendents have the courage to say so publicly for fear of losing even more students to "schools of choice." And teachers' unions, which have historically strengthened public schools and their employees, get blamed for this unfolding situation.

In-depth study tells us that encroaching poverty and the shrinking middle class, rather than teachers' unions, have led to lagging test scores (when compared with those of other countries). When we take poverty out of the equation, our public schools are among the best in the entire world. Clearly, poverty is the problem, not teachers' unions.

Where Did Our Strong Unions Go?

When I was a child, homeless families were unheard of. Now we can't keep up with the need for homeless shelters for entire families. Homeless families, I'm sorry to say, have become the new normal. One thing I'm truly grateful for, though, is that I've never seen a child out on the street begging for food. To a large extent, this is due to the "entitlement" programs that the Republicans are trying to get rid of. I hope the United States never becomes a country where children with empty stomachs are forced to beg for food. Yet sometimes it seems to me that the policies being put in place in Michigan and across the country are leading us in exactly that direction. Please, let's remember the children living in poverty when we make decisions about who will represent us in the legislature.

Since that November night when the Republicans made a clean sweep in Michigan and across the nation, so much has happened. The populace has started to understand that the wealth in this country is zooming toward the wealthiest 1%, at the expense of the shrinking middle class. Every day more people are waking up to the reality of what is happening. As a result, the lies on the extreme right are proliferating.

The first thing that happened after the election is that the war on public employees escalated. Our newly elected leaders (and a few old ones) vilified teachers, firefighters, police officers, and workers risking their lives daily in our prisons. Is it really believable that schoolteachers, firefighters, and social workers created the problems and inequities in our economy? Isn't it possible that those jet-setting around the world to their many homes are more than innocent bystanders to the income inequality making the rich richer and shrinking the middle class? It seems utterly ridiculous to me to put the responsibility on the shoulders of the most brave and generous people in our communities.

But that is what happened. Then, predictably, elected officials began to go after the salaries of public workers.

When Wisconsin governor Scott Walker attacked collective bargaining for public employees, his state's residents took to the streets with prolonged and visible protest marches in the dead of winter in Madison, Wisconsin. At first there were tens of thousands of protesters; eventually one hundred thousand people gathered on the streets around the capital. Most of this was not even discussed in the traditional, corporate media.

When our own Governor Snyder signed the Emergency Manager Law, putting virtual dictators in charge of struggling cities and school districts, Michigan citizens followed Wisconsin's lead. Citizens held rallies at the state capital and across the state, with thousands of people involved. Again and again, our leaders in Michigan ignored the voices of the people.

In Michigan's White Lake area, a group rose up calling itself Reviving Our American Democracy (ROAD). Local teachers organized into the Lakeshore Education Caucus. Statewide, a group of activists formed an organization called

We Are the People. When the protests, letters, e-mails, and phone calls fell on deaf ears in Lansing, this group came together to organize and educate communities. Soon afterward, the national Occupy movement, originally beginning in Wall Street and the business district of New York City, took off and became a protest venue for tens of thousands of young, and not-so-young, people. The Occupy movement spread quickly across the country, including chapters in Grand Rapids, Lansing, and Muskegon. What all these groups have in common is that they are sick of the inequities and injustices built into our economy, which take the greatest toll on hard-working, everyday citizens. They're also sick of the politicians whose policies have created these injustices.

My own experiences in the legislature have proved invaluable as I've joined the movement to revive our stalled democracy. I believe that I have deeper and broader understanding of what is happening to our economy and what it is costing our citizenry. I even believe this insight is possible only because I lost my last campaign.

I love and respect our democracy. But for it to work, we need to open our eyes. Each one of us needs to look for the truth. And when we find top-notch public servants, let's work for them, walk in parades, knock on doors, and make financial donations.

Ross Perot, businessman and presidential candidate in 1992, said we need three things for our democracy to thrive: patriotism, compassion, and hard work. I would add a fourth: honesty. Without it, we are done for.

Epilogue

So what *do* Democrats believe? I can tell you what I believe, as a died-in-the-wool Democrat.

I believe people should work to earn their money, companies should make profits, and those who take risks deserve to make big money. At the same time, I believe it's completely unnecessary—and is damaging to our democracy—for CEOs to get paid 100, 200, or sometimes even 300 times what their average worker is paid. Wouldn't twice as much be enough? Or 10 times more? Or even 50 times more? But 300 times more??? This is absurd, and every thinking person knows it.

This disparity is taking an enormous toll on our democracy. Anyone who points out the absurdity of these inequities immediately becomes lost in a sea of name-calling: socialist, communist, lazy liberal, and so on. I've had my share of name-calling directed at me, and it's possible I'll hear more in the near future, based on the contents of this book.

Some of the 1%, the wealthiest of wealthy citizens, earned their money by the sweat of their brows, and invested wisely. I understand this. But I don't believe that anyone makes it into the top 1% completely on his or her own. Business owners ship their goods on public roads, hire workers educated in public schools, and rely on public safety to protect their property. So why shouldn't those who have been extraordinarily successful pay their fair share for public roads, public schools, public safety, public health, and public libraries—all of which benefit the common good?

Many of the 1% made their money by being born. It took no hard work, courage, or tenacity—they simply were born and inherited it. Not necessarily heroes, they are simply lucky. I don't begrudge them their money—but please, stop painting them as hard working job creators.

I believe in capitalism. I believe that people who work hard should be rewarded. But I also believe that it's critical in a just society to protect our public entities: schools, roads, safety, and health. Many Republican legislators currently setting the agenda for our state don't share my values, or my concern about the common good. They speak eloquently of these issues at campaign time, but then slash funding to public entities. It is as though all public service, in their view, is a form of socialism.

How can these lawmakers call themselves pro-family when their policies harm families, imprison more people, and cut pay for young people trying to support their families?

If, like me, you're concerned about our state, our country, and about politics in general, you need to get involved. Find candidates to support, and support them. Turn off Fox News and MSNBC and do your own research on the issues. And start voting as if your life depended on it—because our lives, and the lives of our children, *do* depend on it. Everyone must have a say. Everyone must vote.

When things are going well, *VOTE*. When they aren't going well, *VOTE*. When you can't figure out who is telling the truth, take the time to figure it out to the best of your ability—then *VOTE*. When you are discouraged, *VOTE*, and if you realize that you have put the wrong person in office, vote differently the next time. But whatever you do, *VOTE*.

People died for that right, and it's the duty of patriots—our privilege *and* our responsibility in a democracy.

Voting is our responsibility, but activism is, too—and sometimes even running for office. Communicating and informing one another of our experiences are our responsibility as well.

I wrote this book both for myself—to document my experiences, positive and negative—and to encourage and inform others who might be considering running for office someday. I wanted everyday citizens to get a better feel for how their democracy works. And, right or wrong, I also wanted to clarify some issues and get a few things off my chest.

It's not the only story from the years that I served in the Michigan House of Representatives. In fact, 110 legislators are serving there, and each one of them has a story about his or her political journey.

Each story is different. This is mine.

About the Author

Mary Valentine lives in Norton Shores, Michigan with her husband of 35 years, Phil Valentine. They are the proud parents of two adult children and two precious granddaughters.

Before running for public office, Mary was a Speech Pathologist in the public school system for many years, most recently in the Reeths-Puffer schools, and a Sunday School teacher. After her children were grown, she became involved in the political process, eventually running for State Representative in the 91st District.

She continues her community engagement through her involvement in Citizens to Preserve Public Education, the Democratic Party, Muskegon Heights Optimist Club, NAACP, Progressive Democratic Women's Caucus and the S. S. Milwaukee Clipper Preservation Board.

She also writes a column on public education issues for the Left of the Line Newsletter and is available for speaking engagements.